EMPOWERED EDUCATORS IN FINLAND

How High-Performing Systems Shape Teaching Quality

Karen Hammerness

Raisa Ahtiainen

Pasi Sahlberg

JB JOSSEY-BASS™

A Wiley Brand

Published by Jossey-Bass
A Wiley Brand

One Montgomery Street, Suite 1000, San Francisco, CA 94104-4594—www.josseybass.com

Jossey-Bass books and products are available through most bookstores. To contact Jossey-Bass directly call our Customer Care Department within the U.S. at 800-956-7739, outside the U.S. at 317-572-3986, or fax 317-572-4002.

Wiley publishes in a variety of print and electronic formats and by print-on-demand. Some material included with standard print versions of this book may not be included in e-books or in print-on-demand. If this book refers to media such as a CD or DVD that is not included in the version you purchased, you may download this material at http://booksupport.wiley.com. For more information about Wiley products, visit www.wiley.com.

ISBN: 9781119369714
ISBN: 9781119372172
ISBN: 9781119372189

Cover design by Wiley
Cover image: © suriya9/Getty Images, Inc.

FIRST EDITION
PB Printingg 10 9 8 7 6 5 4 3 2 1

CONTENTS

FOREWORD

FEW WOULD DISAGREE THAT, among all the factors that affect how much students learn, the quality of their teachers ranks very high. But what, exactly, do policy makers, universities, and school leaders need to do to make sure that the vast majority of teachers in their jurisdiction are *literally* world class?

Perhaps the best way to answer that question is to look carefully and in great detail at what the countries whose students are performing at the world's top levels are doing to attract the highest quality high school students to teaching careers, prepare them well for that career, organize schools so teachers can do the best work of which they are capable, and provide incentives for them to get better at the work before they finally retire.

It was not hard for us to find the right person to lead a study that would do just that. Stanford professor Linda Darling-Hammond is one of the world's most admired researchers. Teachers and teaching have been lifelong professional preoccupations for her. And, not least, Professor Darling-Hammond is no stranger to international comparative studies. Fortunately for us and for you, she agreed to lead an international comparative study of teacher quality in a selection of top-performing countries. The study, *Empowered Educators: How High-Performing Systems Shape Teaching Quality Around the World*, took two years to complete and is unprecedented in scope and scale.

The volume you are reading is one of six books, including case studies conducted in Australia, Canada, China, Finland, and Singapore. In addition to the case studies and the cross-study analysis, the researchers have collected a range of videos and artifacts (http://ncee.org/empowered-educators)—ranging from a detailed look at how the daily schedules of teachers in Singapore ensure ample time for collaboration and planning to a description of the way Shanghai teachers publish their classroom research in refereed journals—that we hope will be of great value to policy makers and educators interested in using and adapting the tools that the top-performing jurisdictions use to get the highest levels of teacher quality in the world.

Studies of this sort are often done by leading scholars who assemble hordes of graduate students to do the actual work, producing reams of reports framed by the research plan, which are then analyzed by the principal investigator. That is not what happened in this case. For this report, Professor Darling-Hammond recruited two lead researcher-writers for each case study, both senior, one from the country being studied and one from another country, including top-level designers and implementers of the systems being studied and leading researchers. This combination of insiders and external observers, scholars and practitioner-policy makers, gives this study a depth, range, and authenticity that is highly unusual.

But this was not just an effort to produce first-class case studies. The aim was to understand what the leaders were doing to restructure the profession of teaching for top performance. The idea was to cast light on that by examining what was the same and what was different from country to country to see if there were common threads that could explain uncommon results. As the data-gathering proceeded, Professor Darling-Hammond brought her team together to exchange data, compare insights, and argue about what the data meant. Those conversations, taking place among a remarkable group of senior policy actors, practitioners, and university-based researchers from all over the world, give this work a richness rarely achieved in this sort of study.

The researchers examined all sorts of existing research literature on the systems they were studying, interviewed dozens of people at every level of the target systems, looked at everything from policy at the national level to practice in individual schools, and investigated not only the specific policies and practices directly related to teacher quality, but the larger economic, political, institutional, and cultural contexts in which policies on teacher quality are shaped.

Through it all, what emerges is a picture of a sea change taking place in the paradigm of mass education in the advanced industrial nations. When university graduates of any kind were scarce and most people had jobs requiring only modest academic skills, countries needed teachers who knew little more than the average high school graduate, perhaps less than that at the primary school level. It was not too hard to find capable people, typically women, to do that work, because the job opportunities for women with that level of education were limited.

But none of that is true anymore. Wage levels in the advanced industrial countries are typically higher than elsewhere in the world. Employers who can locate their manufacturing plants and offices anywhere in the world and who do not need highly skilled labor look for workers who have the basic skills they need in low-wage countries, so the work available to workers with only the basic skills in the high-wage countries is drying up. That process is being greatly accelerated by the rapid advance of automation. The jobs that are left in the high-wage countries mostly demand a higher level of more complex skills.

These developments have put enormous pressure on the governments of high-wage countries to find teachers who have more knowledge and a deeper command of complex skills. These are the people who can get into selective universities and go into occupations that have traditionally had higher status and are better compensated than school teaching. What distinguishes the countries with the best-performing education systems is that: 1) they have figured this out and focused hard on how to respond to these new realities; and 2) they have succeeded not just in coming up with promising designs for the systems they need but in implementing those systems well. The result is not only profound changes in the way they source, educate, train, and support a truly professional teaching force, but schools in which the work of teachers is very differently organized, the demands on school leaders is radically changed, teachers become not the recipient of a new set of instructions from the "center," but the people who are actually responsible for designing and carrying out the reforms that are lifting the performance of their students every day. Not least important, these systems offer real careers in teaching that enable teachers, like professionals in other fields, to gain more authority, responsibility, compensation, and status as they get better and better at the work, without leaving teaching.

This is an exciting story. It is the story that you are holding in your hand. The story is different in every country, province, and state. But the themes behind the stories are stunningly similar. If you find this work only half as compelling as I have, you will be glued to these pages.

MARC TUCKER, PRESIDENT
NATIONAL CENTER ON EDUCATION AND THE ECONOMY

ACKNOWLEDGMENTS

FIRST, WE WANT TO thank the many educators, researchers, policy makers, and faculty in Finland who provided us with their insights, experiences, and expertise through interviews, as well as supplied us with the documents and data for our analysis for this case. A special thank you to the faculty of the Behavioral Sciences at the University of Helsinki: Hannele Cantell, Leena Krokfors, Anu Laine, Markku Jahnukainen, Kalle Juuti, Jari Lavonen, Hannele Niemi, and Auli Toom. We are also grateful to the masters students in teacher education, and the doctoral students, including Lauri Heikonen, who gave their time to help deepen our understanding of teacher preparation and novice teacher support. In addition, the faculty of the Behavioral Sciences at the University of Helsinki graciously hosted Karen as a visiting scholar in June 2014. She is grateful for their hospitality and for the very warm welcome she and her family received during that month.

We also extend a special thank you to the faculty, staff, and students at the Viikki Teacher Training School, University of Helsinki. Schools are busy places, but the teachers, administration, and students made plenty of time for our interviews and helped us understand the important role training schools play in Finnish teacher education. Principal Kimmo Koskinen and Markku Pyysiäinen were generous in not only agreeing to participate in this research but also in helping identify and schedule interviews with their faculty and with teacher education students. Several Viikki teachers not only shared their time in interviews, but also read and responded to drafts of this chapter: we are so grateful to Sirkku Myllyntausta, Anni Loukomies, and Sari Muhonen for their additional support and time.

A number of Finnish teachers were interviewed in the schools where we did our fieldwork and data collection. At the Myllypuro Primary School in Helsinki, we thank Principal Anna Hirvonen, and teachers Jaana Piipponen and Leea Pekkanen. At the Poikkilaakso Primary School, we thank Principal Marja Riitta Rautaparta, and teachers Kirsi-Maria Korhonen and Maria Kuosmanen. At the Langinkoski School in

Kotka, we thank Principal Heidi Honkanen, and teachers Jouni Partanen and Eva Suokko. At the Koulumestari School in Espoo, we thank Principal Vesa Äyräs, Assistant Principal Tiina Korhonen, and teacher Minna Kukkonen, as well as to the Koulumestari students for sharing their work with us; and a special thank you to Jari Lavonen for helping arrange the visit and interviews in Espoo.

We thank the members of the Ministry of Education and Culture, the National Board of Education, and the Trade Union of Education OAJ, including Armi Mikkola, Jouni Kangasniemi, Jussi Pihkala, Irmeli Halinen, and Heljä Misukka. Tanja Steiner answered multiple questions about the VAKAVA exam.

During the analysis and drafting of this case we needed to check facts, dates, and figures. We are especially grateful to Finnish colleagues who read multiple drafts of this case: Auli Toom and Anu Laine both read drafts for accuracy, especially in terms of the descriptions of teacher education. They consistently and patiently responded to a number of follow-up emails we sent as we continued to fill out descriptions and fine-tune our analysis. Close long-term colleagues also read drafts, gave feedback, and checked facts, including Sam Abrams, Thomas Hatch, and Kirsti Klette. Jon Snyder also read several versions and the draft reflects his specific attention to—and understanding of—some of the important contextual but perhaps less immediately visible differences between Finland and the US. Sammi Cannold graciously helped gather and check a series of facts and figures, to support cross-case analysis. As principal investigator, Linda Darling-Hammond gave multiple rounds of feedback throughout the data collection, analysis, and writing. Her probing, thoughtful perspective helped hone and refine the final piece in ways that illuminated critical themes and threads across cases. Lee Shulman's conception of cases, especially his focus upon the question "What is this a case *of*?" also helped guide us as we worked to identify some of the overarching findings, and provided a key foundation for thinking and analysis. While all the analysis and conclusions are ours and we take full responsibility for the writing of this case, our thinking benefited in so many ways from their thoughtfulness and responsive readings.

Throughout the conceptualization, data collection, and analysis, our case benefited from the considered feedback, sustained engagement, and keen analytic perspectives of the other country case authors—Misty Sato and Kai-Ming Cheng (Shanghai); Carol Campbell, Jesslyn Hollar, Ann Lieberman, Pamela Osmond-Johnson, Ken Zeichner, Shane Pisani, and Jacqueline Sohn (Canada); Dion Burns and Ann McIntyre (Australia); and Lin Goodwin and Ee Ling Low (Singapore); and Linda, who is also co-authoring the Singapore and Victoria cases. Our team meetings were not only lively, engaging, and collaborative, but each session strengthened this case and helped surface commonalities as well as features that seem to matter across cases.

Throughout the data collection, analysis, and writing, we relied on the support of the Stanford Center for Opportunity Policy (SCOPE) team, including Dion Burns, Maude Engstrøm, and Sonya Keller, who helped give direction, share materials, advise on ideas, and make connections across cases. Jon Snyder provided leadership, direction, and feedback during the process, and facilitated and guided team meetings in ways that continued to surface insights across researched cases. We gratefully acknowledge the contributions of the Ford Foundation to the aspects of this research addressing the uses of time in the Finnish system. We also offer our thanks to Barnett Berry and the Center for Teaching Quality, whose teachers contributed their experiences and perspectives to this work.

We would not have been able to do this work without the invitation of Linda Darling-Hammond to join this team and to conduct this work, and to have the unique opportunity to dig in and examine in depth the policies of our own focal country as well as of the others in this study.

It's hard to do national and international research without personal support. Karen would like to thank her family, especially her husband Thomas Hatch for his unquestioning support and value for her work, who made it not only possible but easy for her to travel long distances for this research. She is grateful to her three daughters, who never complained about (and always were intrigued by) her trips abroad for data collection, and who all seem to have developed a love for Finnish cabins by the sea. Raisa is grateful to her parents for all the support they have given to her work. Raisa also would like to thank her colleagues, especially Jarkko Hautamäki, Meri Lintuvuori, and Ninja Hienonen at the Centre for Educational Assessment, University of Helsinki, for their consultative help during the process.

ABOUT THE SPONSORING ORGANIZATIONS

THIS WORK IS MADE possible through a grant by the Center on International Education Benchmarking® of the National Center on Education and the Economy® and is part of a series of reports on teacher quality systems around the world. For a complete listing of the material produced by this research program, please visit www.ncee.org/cieb.

The Center on International Education Benchmarking®, a program of NCEE, funds and conducts research around the world on the most successful education systems to identify the strategies those countries have used to produce their superior performance. Through its books, reports, website, monthly newsletter, and a weekly update of education news around the world, CIEB provides up-to-date information and analysis on those countries whose students regularly top the PISA league tables. Visit www.ncee.org/cieb to learn more.

The National Center on Education and the Economy was created in 1988 to analyze the implications of changes in the international economy for American education, formulate an agenda for American education based on that analysis and seek wherever possible to accomplish that agenda through policy change and development of the resources educators would need to carry it out. For more information visit www.ncee.org.

Research for this volume was coordinated by the Stanford Center for Opportunity Policy in Education (SCOPE) at Stanford University. SCOPE was founded in 2008 to foster research, policy, and practice to advance high quality, equitable education systems in the United States and internationally.

ABOUT THE AUTHORS

 **Karen Hammerness**, Ph.D., is the director of Educational Research and Evaluation at the American Museum of Natural History. Her research focuses upon the design and pedagogy of teacher education in the United States and internationally. She is currently co-principal investigator with Dr. Kirsti Klette of the University of Oslo of a study of teacher education program vision and pedagogy in eight programs in five different countries (including Chile, Cuba, Finland, Norway, and the US). Karen is also particularly interested in the nature of teacher education programs that prepare teachers for specific settings (such as Chicago or New York); her coauthored article based upon that work was awarded the 2015 Outstanding Journal of Teacher Education Article from the American Association of Colleges for Teacher Education. Her co-edited book *Inspiring Teaching: Preparing Teachers to Succeed in Mission-Driven Schools* (Harvard Education Press, 2014) shares findings from a longitudinal study of three such context-specific teacher education programs. She has previously contributed chapters about teacher education to a number of books, including *Teacher Education around the World: Changing Policies and Practices* (Routledge, 2012) and *Preparing Teachers for a Changing World* (Jossey-Bass, 2005). She is also the author of a book on teacher's vision entitled *Seeing through Teachers' Eyes: Professional Ideals and Classroom Practices* (Teachers College Press, 2006). As director of Educational Research and Evaluation at the American Museum of Natural History, her research agenda is focused upon educator and youth learning in both formal and informal settings. In particular, she is interested in how educators in both formal and informal settings learn to teach to high standards and how children come to develop an identity as a scientist.

 **Raisa Ahtiainen,** MA (in Education) and special education needs teacher, works as project researcher at the Centre for Educational Assessment (CEA), University of Helsinki, where she is involved with research projects concerning educational reform, teachers' professional development, and various education-related development initiatives. She became a member of CEA's research team in 2010 through her masters' thesis, which was linked to their project of that time, "Special Education Reform, Evaluation, and Development." Recently Raisa finished a study examining an initiative promoting issues of diversity and multiculturalism in Finnish schools. In 2015 she also worked as a field researcher in the evaluation of Finnish Ministry of Foreign Affairs' development cooperation concerning inclusive education, which was coordinated by Development Portfolio Management Group at University of Southern California. In addition, she is one of the authors in a newly published book called *"Erityisopetuksesta oppimisen ja koulunkäynnin tukeen"* [From Special Education to Support to Learning and School Attendance]; her chapter explores Special Education Reform (2011) in light of Finnish education system's structure. Today, alongside her work at the CEA, Raisa is finalizing her postgraduate research that analyzes the implementation process of recent Special Education Reform.

 **Pasi Sahlberg** is a Finnish educator, author, and scholar. He has worked as schoolteacher, teacher educator, researcher, and policy advisor in Finland and has studied education systems and reforms around the world. He has also served the World Bank in Washington, DC; European Commission in Torino, Italy: and OECD as an external expert. His core expertise is in teacher education, international education policies, higher education, and educational leadership. He has published widely about educational change and improvement, and his book *Finnish Lessons 2.0: What Can the World Learn from Educational Change in Finland* won the 2013 Grawemeyer Award. He also received the Education Award in Finland in 2012, the Robert Owen Award in Scotland in 2014, the Lego Prize in 2016, and the Rockefeller Foundation Bellagio Residency in 2017. He is a former director general of CIMO at the Finland's Ministry of Education and Culture in Helsinki and a visiting Professor of Practice at Harvard University's Graduate School of Education.

He is currently an international speaker and advisor to the governments of Scotland, Sweden, Malta, and Finland and a visiting professor at the Arizona State University in the United States, adjunct professor at the University of Helsinki, and member of the Governing Board of the University of Oulu. His latest book is *Hard Questions on Global Educational Change* (2017). Twitter: @pasi_sahlberg.

ONLINE DOCUMENTS AND VIDEOS

Access online documents an videos at
http://ncee.org/empowered-educators

Link Number	Description	URL
1	Finland Futures Education	http://ncee.org/2017/01/finland-futures-education/
2	Finland Basic Education Act 1998	http://ncee.org/2017/01/finland-basic-education-act-1998/
3	Finnish Teacher Education Decree	http://ncee.org/2017/01/finnish-teacher-education-decree/
4	Video: Pasi Sahlberg on Teacher Recruitment	http://ncee.org/2016/12/video-pasi-sahlberg-on-teacher-recruitment/
5	Video: Finnish Teacher Training School	http://ncee.org/2016/12/video-finnish-teacher-training-school/
6	Audio: Sirkku Myllyntausta	http://ncee.org/2016/12/audio-sirkku-myllyntausta/
7	Audio: Anu Laine, Part 1	http://ncee.org/2016/12/audio-anu-laine-part-1/
8	Audio: Anu Laine, Part 2	http://ncee.org/2016/12/audio-anu-laine-part-2/
9	Video: Pasi Sahlberg on Curriculum	http://ncee.org/2016/12/video-pasi-sahlberg-on-curriculum/
10	Finnish Teacher Education Decree	http://ncee.org/2017/01/finnish-teacher-education-decree/
11	Finland Education and Research Development Plan 2011-2016	http://ncee.org/2017/01/finland-education-and-research-development-plan-2011-2016/
12	Finland Basic Education Decree	http://ncee.org/2017/01/finland-basic-education-decree/

Access online documents and videos at
http://www.routledge.com/...

Introduction

Upon the occasion of the birth of a new baby in Finland, since the 1930's, the Finnish government has been providing every new mother with a cardboard box filled with clothes, sheets, toys, diapers, and other essential items. The box even includes a small mattress, and the box can actually (and often does for many newborns) serve as a simple crib.[1] The intention of the box is to ensure that all children in Finland have an equal start; but it serves also as a symbol of the centrality of equity and children in Finland (Lee, 2014). This rather simple, straightforward tradition is also illustrative of the Finnish policy context that we explore in this case—one that is focused upon equity and a strong early start, and centered around children.

In this book, we examine the policies and practices that have been deliberately developed to support and contribute to a national policy context that is centered upon children: a policy context that builds capacity for quality teaching. Upon first glance, one might quickly conclude that the strong and equitable student outcomes in Finland are simply the result of recruiting top candidates into teaching. Or, some might wonder whether the small size and relative homogeneity of Finland makes it more likely for all children to achieve at the high levels they do. Similarly, one might hear about the respect and value for the teaching profession in Finland; and respond, "we can't replicate that here in the United States [or in any other country], it's just part of Finnish culture."

However, we tell a story of intentional, considered decision making that has taken place in Finland over just a few decades. We show that the Finnish government, the Ministry of Education and Culture, the Finnish National Board of Education, and other actors at all levels of the educational system have carried out a set of considered, deliberate policy choices and created multiple practical supports that function in concert, which intersect in Finland to create a coherent, strong, and equitable educational context. In turn, these policies function to build capacity (and continue to do so) at multiple levels of the system to produce well-prepared, committed, reflective, and responsible teachers. The deliberate work to focus upon capacity building of the teaching profession is far from the result simply recruiting the cream of the crop into teaching or "just the culture." Furthermore, it is not true that Finland's small size (about five and a half million people [Statistics Finland, 2014b]) and relative homogeneity means that we can't apply what we can learn from Finland. While of course there are cultural, societal, and political features that we cannot replicate, what we can learn from Finland has to do with the intentional and deliberate choice to emphasize the thorough preparation and training of teachers, the development of a high-quality workforce of teachers, and purposeful efforts to eliminate differences in student achievement.

These carefully aligned and consistent policy choices, which include efforts to develop strong academic, research-based teacher preparation, to support and promote the work of teaching, to make high quality teaching and education available to all Finnish children, to address issues of equity and diversity, and to carefully and gradually build a more inclusive school system for all children, have created a coherent context for an educational system that has been successful in producing strong student results on international tests such as OECD's PISA and IEA's TIMSS and PIRLS.

One particularly impressive feature of the strong outcomes is the remarkable equity in achievement in Finland. Indeed, in Finland, the effect of socioeconomic status has far less impact on reading, science, and mathematics achievement than in other countries (interestingly, socio-economic status also seems to have little relationship to the problem-solving skills of *adults* in Finland, as well). In their most recent release of findings, the OECD reports that Finland, alongside countries like Australia, Canada, and the Netherlands, "combine high levels of performance with equity in education opportunities (OECD, 2012). It is also important that income inequality in Finland is one of the lowest among OECD countries (OECD, 2012; Sahlberg, 2011). As Figure 1 shows, this income equality may contribute to high achievement in reading, mathematics, and science. However, Finland far out performs several other similarly equitable nations.

However, it is also critically important to understand that success in Finland means much more than the narrow range of learning outcomes that are captured in high PISA scores. Finland ranks among the top four countries[2] on measures of children's well-being (UNICEF, 2007, 2013). A recent OECD report examining the skills of adults found Finnish adults had excellent literacy and numeracy skills; and Finnish adults were among the top in their ability to solve problems in a technology rich environment (OECD, 2013).[3] In a report recently initiated by the United Nations, Finland ranked among the top ten countries in terms of a number of important features identified as central to positive human development—key measures of well-being including safety, physical and mental health, and economic measures. *Equity* was one of the

Figure 1   Income inequality (gini coefficient) and
aggregated student achievement (PISA score average
of all three domains) in OECD countries in 2012
(OECD, 2013b).

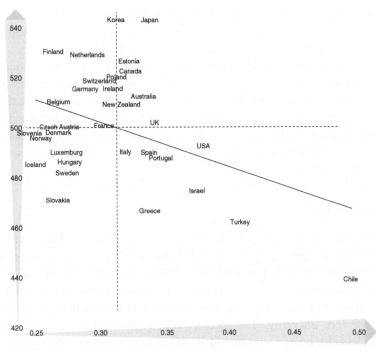

distinguishing factors that separated countries like Finland and Norway and The Netherlands that scored high on all these measures; while countries that scored lower also had indications of "loss of human potential due to inequity" (United Nations, 2014).

In this climate, teachers are not only respected and valued, but the corps of teachers is effectively—and continually—sustained at a high level of professionalism. Further, such intentional investment in high quality teachers has a positive economic impact, teacher retention is higher across the profession in Finland than in countries like the United States—meaning that school districts and communities do not have to invest in the costly process of recruiting and training new teachers as often as every year. There is no Finnish term for teacher retention (Itkonen & Jahnukainen, 2007). Finnish teachers' commitment to their profession has been extremely high: a national survey of 4,500 Finnish teachers found that only about 10% of

Finnish teachers leave their positions (Jokinen et al. 2013, p. 36). Indeed, that survey suggested that almost three of four teachers were convinced that they would remain in teaching until retirement. In that same survey, only about 20% of teachers reported that they have considered leaving teaching for another profession (ibid, p. 36; see also Heikonen et al., in press). Recent TALIS data may shed some light upon these findings: in Finland, 95% of middle school teachers report that the more positive aspects of their work outweigh any negative elements (OECD, 2013).

We begin with providing some background on the overall context of Finland and Finnish teachers; the policy context that supports and contributes to teacher quality; and then describe in detail the way these policies, supports, and decisions play out to support quality teaching from preparation through to professional practice—reflecting a kind of "continuum of teaching" described by scholars of teaching like Feiman-Nemser (2001).

The Context

Finland is divided into about 300 local municipalities that have the main responsibility to organize education for their citizens according to national regulations and legislation. The challenge Finland has with its decentralized and locally controlled education system is related to the relatively large land area that is inhabited by less than six million people very unevenly. The metropolitan region, including the capital city Helsinki, hosts about one-fifth of Finland's entire population. Many issues affecting teachers and schools in Finland today, such as increasing immigration, tightening public budgets, and access to professional development for teachers, are therefore not seen in the same ways in different parts of the country.

Education is mostly funded by local municipal taxes in Finland. Because the wealth of Finnish municipalities varies greatly, the proportion of central government's share of education spending is different from one municipality to another. The Finnish National Board of Education uses an equalizing formula, however, that takes into account specific needs of the region as well as attends to any differences in wealth, so that districts all gain the support they need. Some districts are fully supported by government subsidies while others are able to support their work through some municipal funding. This calculation and effort to equalize funding means that the wealthier districts do not end up with an unequally high proportion of funding. Roughly speaking, two thirds of school education spending in Finland comes from local funds and the rest from the central government's budget. Government's subsidies to municipalities are not earmarked—which means that locally elected politicians and school boards in municipalities decide how the overall local budgets will allocate resources to education and other public services.

Finland's municipalities have also a degree of freedom in terms of education administration and governance. For example, school principals are normally appointed by municipal councils and their politically appointed boards of education. In some cases teachers may also be recruited by the municipalities but in many other situations, teachers apply directly to open vacancies in schools. By law municipalities are required to monitor the quality of education including teachers' and principals' performance in schools but without national framework or common procedures.

There are three national institutions that play a normative, regulatory role with locally governed school system in Finland. First, Ministry of Education and Culture (MOEC) is part of Finland's government that is in charge of all education in Finland as well as culture, youth, and athletics. The Ministry with its two ministers has three broad responsibilities within its education remit: Assist the Parliament in legislative framework, develop national education policy, and guarantee sufficient budget within state's annual budget and how it will be allocated to various aspects within education system. Second, the Finnish National Board of Education (FNBE) as a state agency operates as an administrative, semi-independent bureau assisting the Ministry in its tasks and supporting municipalities and schools in their work. The board has also three main responsibilities nationally, namely development of national curriculum frameworks for all school types, evaluation of quality of education, and providing support services to teachers, the roughly 3,000 schools including comprehensive schools and upper secondary. Third, the Finnish Education Evaluation Centre (FINEEC) carries out evaluations related to education including the operations of education providers from early childhood education to higher education. The centre comprises an Evaluation Council, a Higher Education Evaluation Committee, and units for the evaluation of general education, vocational education and training (VET), and higher education (see Figure 2). This diagram also shows the important relationship of OAJ and Kuntaliito in educational governance. The Trade Union of Education in Finland (or, OAJ) is a professional association for teachers, and plays an important role not only in areas such as contract negotiations, but also in being a public voice around educational issues. Ninety-five percent of Finnish teachers belong to the

Figure 2   Levels of Government in the Finnish
Educational System

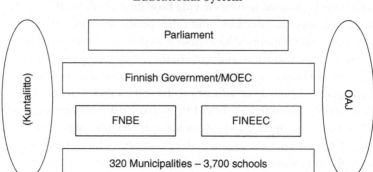

OAJ (Sahlberg, 2015). Finally, Kuntaliito is the association of Finnish Local and Regional Authorities.

With its high levels of educational achievement and attainment, Finland is regarded as one of the world's most literate societies. Just as the baby box of supplies for new parents signifies attention to an equal start for infants in Finland, Finland offers an equally good start to schooling for every child: A long parental leave system guarantees that parents can remain home with the child until the infant is one year old. Children in Finland have a subjective right to high-quality and safe early childhood programs that are heavily subsidized by public authorities. All children are required to attend publically funded preschool beginning at the age of six (a year of preschool; half-days). It is perhaps no wonder that 99% of the age cohort complete compulsory basic education; and 94% of those who start the academic strand of upper secondary school graduate. Completion rates in vocational upper secondary school also reach close to 90% (Statistics Finland, 2014b; Välijärvi & Sahlberg, 2008). Since it emerged in 2000 as the top-scoring OECD nation on the international PISA assessments, researchers have been pouring into the country to study the "Finnish miracle."

How did a country with an undistinguished education system in the 1970s surge to the head of the global class in just few decades? Indeed, until the 1960s the level of educational attainment in Finland remained rather low. Only 1 out of 10 adult Finns in that time had completed more than nine years of basic education; achieving a university degree was an uncommon attainment (Sahlberg, 2015). Back then, the education level of the nation was comparable to that of Malaysia or Peru, and lagged behind its Scandinavian neighbors, Denmark, Norway, and Sweden. At the same time, the teaching profession was always valued in Finland,[4] as it was in most other countries until then. Yet what is significant in Finland is that whereas in most other countries teaching has gradually lost its attractiveness among young people and social status in society, Finland has been able to maintain and even strengthen them.

These educational accomplishments seem all the more remarkable given that Finnish children do not start primary school until age seven. The educational system in Finland today consists of a pre-school year at age six (half-day), followed by nine-year basic school—a six-year primary school and a three-year lower secondary school (junior high school)—compulsory to all. Typically children attend their neighborhood school; and the drop-out rate is very low (about .07%) (Graham & Jahnukainen, 2011). This is followed by a voluntary three-year upper secondary education with two streams: general and vocational education. Subject-focused teachers (who typically have expertise in one-two subject areas such as math and physics or physical education and health) provide instruction in the upper grades of basic school (grades 7, 8, and 9) as well as at the upper-secondary level. Principals determine the assignment of teachers in these upper grades: the assignment of subject teachers depends upon school needs in terms of subject areas and number of pupils. This system serves about 1.2 million students who are currently in basic to university education (Statistics Finland, 2014b).

The Finnish education system does not employ external standardized student testing to drive the performance of schools; neither does it employ a rigorous external inspection system (Kumpulainen & Lankinen, 2012). In Finland, as in other Nordic countries like Norway, there is no word for "accountability" in the education vocabulary (Hatch, 2015). In Finland, the focus of teachers is upon a sense of "responsibility" (Sahlberg, 2015). Instead of test-based accountability, the Finnish system relies on the expertise and personal investment of teachers who are knowledgeable and committed to their students. Although it may seem counterintuitive to Americans accustomed to external testing as a means of accountability, Finland's leaders point to its use of school-based, student-centered, open-ended tasks embedded in the curriculum (Link 1) as an important reason for the nation's extraordinary success on international student assessments (Lavonen, 2008; Finnish National Board of Education, 2007).

Among young Finns, teaching is consistently the most admired profession in regular opinion polls of high school graduates (Liiten, 2004;

Martin & Pennanen, 2015; see also Ministry of Education and Culture, 2012). Becoming a primary school teacher in Finland is a very competitive process, and only Finland's strongest students are able to fulfill those professional dreams. Every spring, thousands of high school graduates submit their applications to the Departments of Teacher Education in eight Finnish universities. It is not sufficient to complete high school and pass a rigorous matriculation examination. While successful candidates must have high academic achievement, what is often overlooked in discussions of Finnish teacher education is that the system is designed with multiple recruitment strategies. The range of strategies to identify potential teachers reflects the belief that a holistic view of ideal candidates will yield the best teachers. There are a number of aspects of selection, some of which emphasize academic preparation and while others emphasize, for instance, interpersonal and relational skills. These abilities are assessed not only in a competitive interview process but also in their ability to interpret and understand real educational research. Desirable Finnish teachers are not only those who have academic strength, but who also excel in art, music, dance, drama, or other arenas as well. Annually only about 1 in every 10 applicants will be accepted to study to become a teacher in Finnish primary schools, for example. Among all categories of teacher education, about 5,000 teachers are selected from about 20,000 applicants.

Without a set of policies designed to build capacity around quality teaching and equitable practices, Finland's current international success would have been impossible. Today, Finland publicly recognizes the value of its teachers and trusts their professional judgment in schools. Finns regard teaching as a noble, prestigious profession—akin to medicine, law, or economics—and one driven by moral purpose rather than material interests. But this is *not* simply the result of recruiting the very best for teaching in public schools nor of a tacit cultural value for teaching. Rather, the respect for teachers has emerged in direct relationship to the sustained and pointed efforts of policy makers, educators, and other government actors in Finland who have made a set of decisions that led to the development and support of a continuum of teacher preparation and ultimately to a quality teaching corps. In 2009, for instance, the Ministry of Education documents reiterated this intention: "The aim [of Finnish education policy] is a coherent policy geared to educational equity and a high level of education among the population as a whole. The principle of lifelong learning entails that everyone has sufficient learning skills and opportunities to develop their knowledge and skills in different learning environments throughout their lifespan." This case underscores the coherent nature of that policy and its relationship to teaching quality.

A policy context aiming for equity and "education for all." Overall, Finnish education policy has been developed to reflect a belief in "education for all"—in other words, an investment in the idea that every person has the right and the ability to an education of the highest level they wish, at no cost (Rinne, Kivirauma, & Lehtinen 2004). This expansive policy is rooted in a vision of what some have termed the "Nordic model" which rests upon four basic principles: equity, participation, flexibility, and progressiveness (Antikainen, 2006). At the same time, Finnish policy makers have also taken a measured, careful approach to enacting such policies; rather than seeking short-term impact, they have taken a long view that requires step-by-step work to achieve their goals. For instance, shifting the system from a parallel organization that served children with severe needs separately took several decades to change and required a number of intentional but gradual shifts in both school practices and teacher preparation (Tuunainen, 1994; Sabel, Saxenian, Miettinen, Kristensen, & Hautamäki, 2010). Similarly, rapidly increasing immigration of children who speak languages other than Finnish has also substantially affected how teachers are trained and supported in schools since the 1990s—but the Finnish system has been adjusting in response.

Several key steps included the Comprehensive School Act of 1970 (CSA, 1970), in which the aim was to address broad social reform, especially equitable access to opportunities, through educational change. The first change to occur was the gradual integration of two strands of schools (grades 4–9) into one comprehensive school system of grades 1–9, informed by the principles of equal education for all students (Aho, Pitkanen, & Sahlberg, 2006). The intention was to create a system in which all children would be served. For instance, in the case of children with special needs, this meant that *schools* would be responsible for children with the most severe special needs—as opposed to the social welfare system. However, like most of these educational policy developments in Finland, these changes were enacted slowly and deliberately—so the change was designed to start by including children with moderate special needs (Jahnukainen & Korhonen, 2003).

The next major step was the Basic Education Act of 1998 (Link 2) (BEA, 1998). The purpose of the Basic Education Act was to more coherently align legislation and policy around schooling, and to provide more flexible and responsive legislation. It brought together a large number of laws, bylaws, and acts in a more holistic education law. For instance, it enhanced the transition points between various levels of education—primary, lower secondary, and upper secondary education. Among other shifts, the BEA initiated the practices of IEP's such that children with even severe needs could be placed in regular classrooms. As Graham and Jahnukainen (2011, p. 276) report, "In practice, all these changes mean that currently every child—*including those with a disability*—has the right to enroll in their local school." As the number of students with special needs served by the comprehensive schools increased, "both the number of special schools and special school placements has been decreasing over time." Furthermore, amendments to the Basic Education Act in 2011 have recently directed the language even more towards the *pedagogical* in contrast to the previous *medical* language; decreasing the use of "special" terms and increasing support-related expressions. Currently the Finnish comprehensive schools emphasize the concept of "support for learning and school attendance" instead of "special education" (Thuneberg, Vainikainen, Ahtiainen, Lintuvuori, Salo, & Hautamäki, 2013; Thuneberg, Hautamäki, Ahtiainen, Lintuvuori, Vainikainen, & Hilasvuori, 2014).

In this next section, we dive deeply into the first layer of the policy context designed to support quality teaching: teacher preparation.

Finnish Policies and Practices of Teacher Education

Finland has no alternative routes into teaching. Only eight institutions prepare teachers in Finland for K–12 schools; they are all research universities. Indeed, shifting the responsibility for teacher preparation to the purview of universities came in 1971 through a teacher training law and it has remained there ever since (Uusiautti & Määttä, 2013). Prior to 1971, primary school teachers were prepared in teachers colleges or special teacher education seminars, while lower and upper school teachers were prepared in subject specific areas within Finnish universities. In 1967, however, as part of the movement towards comprehensive education, a Teacher Training Committee put forth the proposition that universities should provide teacher education; by 1969, the Committee on Teacher Education had begun the "painful process" of closing remaining elementary school teacher training programs (Uusiautti & Määttä, 2013). As a result of formal decrees put in place in the 1970s (and affirmed in 1995, and again in 2005), only universities offer teacher education (Link 3). By 1978–1979, new degree requirements mandated that all teachers would need to possess a master's degree in order to teach (Kansanen, 2012; Krokfors, 2007; Jakku-Sihvonen & Niemi, 2006; see also Uusiautti & Määttä, 2013).[5] Alongside this key decision to make teacher education solely the concern of the university, there are several other unique features of teacher preparation that contribute directly to the capacity of the country to create a strong and quality teacher workforce: a focus upon primary education as the basis for a strong teacher corps; a strongly academic and research-based curriculum; the emphasis upon teacher training schools as carefully developed sites for learning to teach; and a support for teaching as a valuable resource at all levels of the system, including even at the university faculty level.

A unique emphasis upon preparing primary education teachers. Reflective of the investment in early education in Finland, acceptance into preparation programs for the primary level is not only more competitive but also requires even more comprehensive preparation. In this case, we elaborate the preparation to teach at the primary level, to illustrate the extensive nature of the university coursework required as well as the clinical preparation. Preparation to teach at the lower-secondary level (grades 7–9) and upper-secondary level (grades 9–13) is organized somewhat differently, requiring extensive preparation as well in both subject area and pedagogy, but not to quite the same degree as that for teachers in the primary grades. Teaching kindergarten (ages 0–6) requires a bachelor's degree. Since Finnish children are not required to attend school until age six (pre-school at age six and school at age seven or in the autumn of the year when a child turns seven; the same applies to preschool that starts in the autumn of the year when the child turns six), preparation for Finnish kindergarten teachers is considered to be somewhat separate. Prospective kindergarten teachers are also required attend one of the eight universities that prepare teachers—they are the only sites for teacher preparation at all levels.

Entrance exams for prospective teachers: The VAKAVA as a tool for equity. At the primary level, all of those candidates interested in entering teacher education and becoming teachers at the primary level (or class teachers, for grades 1–6, or children from ages 7–13) must first take a demanding exam called the VAKAVA which is overseen by a governing board that makes all the administrative decisions as well as a work group that selects the articles and draws up questions for the exam (for more information see University of Helsinki, 2014).[6] The governing board consists of one representative from all the eight universities that prepare teachers—usually the representative is the faculty member responsible for the program. In addition, there is one representative (a faculty member or lecturer in teacher education) as well from each of the eight universities on the working group—the group responsible for both creating as well as grading the exams. The equity-based rationale behind developing the exam was to ensure that all upper secondary students who wished to be considered could have access to the highly competitive profession. The guiding philosophy behind the exam is captured by the Finnish term "samalta viivalta" which means equal opportunity—

suggesting everyone stands at the same starting line when starting the exam—and underscores the notion that everyone should have the same opportunity to apply to the program. The VAKAVA, which was first administered in 2006, consists of a set of five to eight educational research articles—new articles are selected each year—which are released as a book in March each year (see Figure 3). The articles included are peer-reviewed research articles that have been published over the prior year, in a variety of educational journals. In 2013, for example, the VAKAVA included seven articles—among them a study that examined children's discourse in mathematics classrooms, and research that investigated children's use of social media and how they portrayed themselves to others. Candidates have approximately six weeks to read the materials and complete the exam, which is given in May.[7]

Candidates must read all research articles thoroughly, and answer multiple choice questions that are intended to draw upon candidates' skills of inference and analysis. Members of the board who prepare the VAKAVA describe their efforts to develop questions for the exam that are not simply rote or routine, but that require application and analysis. For instance, on the most recent VAKAVA, candidates were asked to examine a chart that was similar to—but not included in—one of the articles, and to interpret the chart based upon the analyses that had been done in the article. In other words, they had to make inferences and to engage in an analysis of new data for the exam (see Figure 4).

Concurrent with the VAKAVA, candidates indicate which university's primary teacher education program they would like to attend—whether they wish to attend the University of Turku or the University of Helsinki, for instance. Once the exam period is over, the institutions get a list of those candidates in terms of their scores on the exam and can select among those who attain the highest scores on the VAKAVA to accept into primary teacher education. This past year, over seven thousand Finnish students took the VAKAVA, seeking one of the 660 available spots in primary teacher education (University of Helsinki, 2014).

There is a high level of interest in primary teacher education. In 2013, for example, there was a record number of applicants to primary teacher education. More than 8,000 applicants applied for about 800 available spots in Finnish universities, for the primary teacher education programs. In that same year, there were nearly 1,800 applicants for 120 spots in Helsinki's primary teacher education program (Sahlberg, 2015). This interest has continued; this past year the Helsinki faculty had 1,649 applicants who took the VAKAVA exam and accepted only a little under 7% of those who took the VAKAVA for those 120 spots (Personal

Figure 3   Cover of VAKAVA Exam Book

communication, Tanja Steiner, 2015). A recent report released by Statistics Finland (2013) found that "initial teacher training has grown in popularity" and that the number of applicants in Finland for elementary teacher education has increased by 18%, since the last survey done in

Figure 4   Sample VAKAVA Question

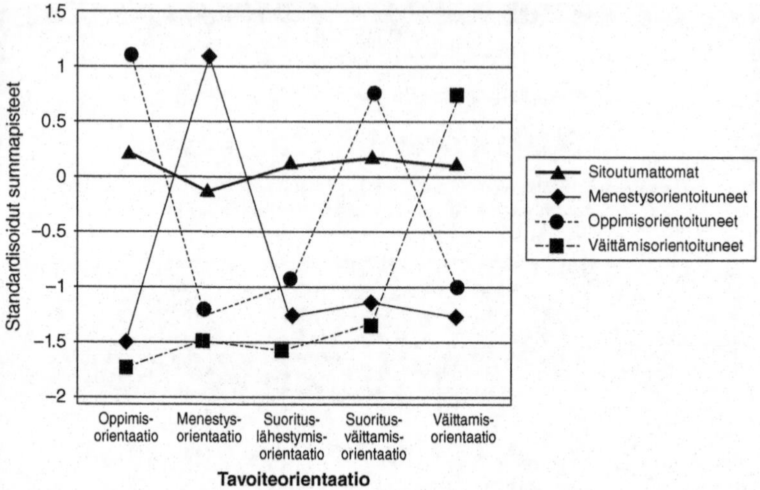

2010 (Finnish National Board of Education, 2014a). In response, programs have increased their intake so that essentially the number of places remain available, but clearly, competition for admission to primary or elementary teacher education programs is extremely high (Link 4).

Further selection into primary education: Interviews for a selected group. However, simply passing the VAKAVA with a high score does not guarantee admission into the competitive primary teacher education programs in Finland; there are multiple selection strategies that aim to identify teachers that are informed by a broad view of what makes a good teacher. Interviews, which enable faculty to assess interpersonal skills and other important skills such as musical or artistic talent, are a key part of the selection process. In 2012, for instance, at the University of Helsinki, the faculty chose 360 students who achieved the highest scores on the VAKAVA and identified a little under half for interviews, which was the next step in their selection process. There is no common interview protocol or other selection procedure between different universities: universities have the freedom to decide what selection process they would like to use in order to select candidates. At the University of Helsinki, those carefully selected candidates then were interviewed both individually and in groups by professors and lecturers of the Department of Teacher Education. In the group interview, 3–4 candidates are given a text to read, or an illustration about teachers and their work, and to prepare to discuss together how they might introduce and discuss it in a group situation. The group of prospective candidates are observed by teacher educators, who are watching for motivation, willingness to work together, and other characteristics. Teacher educators also then interview the candidates individually, and rank order their choices. Ultimately, 120 are chosen for acceptance into the program. Those who are not successful in being accepted often apply again next year after gaining experience in working in schools and taking additional coursework. In 2014, 56% of the examinees (who responded to the VAKAVA's survey of participants) reported taking the VAKAVA for the first time, but 28% reported taking it a second time, and 12% the third time (Tanja Steiner, personal communication). If students do not succeed on the VAKAVA exam, one common alternative is to apply to kindergarten teacher education (preparation to work the youngest children, ages 0–6) or subject teacher education for secondary level teaching where the competition at entry is not so fierce. (However, prospective candidates would then still need to complete studies in a particular discipline in order to be eligible for this option.)

The curriculum for primary teacher preparation. Having completed this challenging process of competing for acceptance, and offered a position at the university of the candidates' choice, class teacher candidates then proceed through five years of preparation—three years of undergraduate work, followed by two years of master's degree coursework.

For a primary school teacher (in Finland they are referred to as "class teachers") qualification, students must complete coursework in the disciplines (which includes not only Finnish, mathematics, history, and science, but also drama, music, physical education); pedagogical coursework; coursework on communication and language development; and coursework in research and analysis (which also includes the writing of both a bachelor's and master's degree theses) (see Figure 5).

Candidates take considerable preparation in each of their subject areas. For instance, during the first year of the primary teacher education program, referred to as CLASS teacher education in Finland, students are taking rigorous coursework in the teaching of different subject areas that they will eventually teach from: Finnish to chemistry to mathematics. Simultaneously, students must take pedagogical courses including a methods (or didactics) course; two courses on child development (tailored for teaching specifically, loosely translated as "Interacting with and Awareness of Pupils" and "Introduction to Educational Psychology"); and engage in a series of gradually lengthening placements in the training school. During those initial visits, student-teachers are learning how to observe children through assignments that require them to chart social relationships, to interview children, and to apply what they are learning in their child development courses. They are also asked

Figure 5   Curriculum for Class Teacher Education 2012–2015

HELSINGIN YLIOPISTO
HELSINGFORS UNIVERSITET
UNIVERSITY OF HELSINKI

Curriculum for Class Teacher Education 2012-2015
300 ECTS credits
BEd= studies included in the Bachelor of Education degree
MEd= studies included in the Master of Education degree

		BEd	MEd
Communication Studies and Orienting Studies	**25 CR**		
Basics of Curriculum Planning	**2 cr**	1 cr	1 cr
Language and Communication Skills	**14 cr**		
Mother Tongue			
Speech Communication and Interaction Skills		2 cr	
Drama Pedagogy		3 cr	
Scientific Writing			3 cr
Foreign Language		3 cr	
Second National Language		3 cr	
Education and Social Justice	**3 cr**	3 cr	
Information and Communication Technology in Learning	**3 cr**	3 cr	
Introduction to Media Education	**3 cr**		3 cr
Main Subject Studies in Education	**140 cr**		
Cultural Bases of Education	**16 cr**		
Introduction to Educational Sciences		3 cr	
Social, Historical and Philosophical Foundations of Education		4 cr	
Facing Specificity and Multiplicity / Education for Diversities		6 cr	
Cultural Diversity in Schools			3 cr
Psychological Bases of Education	**11 cr**		
Introduction to Educational Psychology		5 cr	
Interaction and Awareness of Pupil		6 cr	
Pedagogical Bases of Education	**23 cr**		
Didactics		7 cr	
Theory and Didactics of Early Childhood Education		3 cr	
Evaluation and Ethics of Teaching and Learning		3 cr	
Curriculum Theory and Evaluation			3 cr
Pedagogical Knowing and Construction of Personal Practical Theory			7 cr
Research Studies in Education	**70 cr**		
Introduction to Educational Research		3 cr	
Quantitative Research Methods		4 cr	
Qualitative Research Methods		3 cr	
Bachelor's Thesis (incl. seminars 4 cr)		10 cr	
either Practicing Research Methods (quantitative)			4 cr
or Practicing Research Methods (qualitative)			4 cr
Methodtray (two optional advanced method courses depending on one's own needs)			3+3=6 cr
Master's Thesis			40 cr
Teaching Practice	**20 cr**		
Orienting Practicum		3 cr	
Minor Subject Practicum			9 cr
Master Practicum			8 cr

Department of Teacher Education
Faculty of Behavioural Sciences

HELSINGIN YLIOPISTO
HELSINGFORS UNIVERSITET
UNIVERSITY OF HELSINKI

	BEd	MEd
Minor Subject Studies		
Multidisciplinary Studies in Subjects and Cross-curricular Issues taught in Comprehensive School	**60 cr**	
1. Mother Tongue and Literature Education	8 cr	8 cr
2. Mathematics Education	7 cr	7 cr
3. Arts and Skills Education	14 cr	
3.1 Visual Arts Education		3 cr
3.2 Craft Education		5 cr
3.3 Didactics of Physical Education		3 cr
3.4 Music Education		3 cr
4. Didactics in Humanistic Subjects	6 cr	
4.1 History Education		3 cr
either 4.2 a) Lutheran Religious Education		3 cr
or 4.2 b) Secular Ethics Education		3 cr
5. Didactics in Environmental and Science Subjects	12 cr	
5.1 Geography Education		3 cr
5.2 Biology Education		3 cr
5.3 Physics Education		3 cr
5.4 Chemistry Education		3 cr
6, 7 & 8. Optional Courses	13 cr	
One of the following:		
6.1 Visual Arts Education, Pedagogical Orientation		4 cr
6.2 Physical Education, Pedagogical Orientation		4 cr
6.3 Music Education, Pedagogical Orientation		4 cr
6.4 & 6.5 Craft Education, Pedagogical Orientation		4 cr
and one of the following:		
6.6 Visual Arts Education, Socio-cultural Orientation		3 cr
6.7 Physical Education, Socio-cultural Orientation		3 cr
6.8 Music Education, Socio-cultural Orientation		3 cr
6.9 Craft Education, Socio-cultural Orientation		3 cr
One of the following:		
7.1 History Education, Optional Studies		3 cr
7.2 Religious Education, Lutheranism, Optional Studies		3 cr
7.3 Secular Ethics Education, Optional Studies		3 cr
One of the following:		
8.1 Geography Education, Optional Studies		3 cr
8.2 Biology Education, Optional Studies		3 cr
8.3 Physics Education, Optional Studies		3 cr
8.4 Chemistry Education, Optional Studies		3 cr
Optional Minor Subject and Optional Studies	**75 cr**	40 cr 35 cr
Study points in the whole degree:	**300 CR**	

1 ECTS credit = 27 hours of work

Department of Teacher Education
Faculty of Behavioural Sciences

to observe teachers' teaching and classroom interactions. Students are simultaneously taking coursework in the teaching of all the subjects that they will eventually teach (60 credits)—they also typically choose to take a certain number of "pure" content courses (such as mathematics or Finnish) as part of their "minor subject" and "optional studies" (75 credits). This preparation—with a focus upon the *teaching* of subject matter rather than "pure" content courses—differs from preparation of secondary teachers and has been in place since the late 1970s (Uusiautti & Määttä, 2013). In primary teacher education, students study their subject only if they specialize in it (for example, mathematics) as a minor subject—although it is quite common for primary teachers to select a subject for specialization. Otherwise, the content studies have both a multidisciplinary and educational focus—so that the content is studied through a lens of teaching or, as one might argue, as pedagogical content knowledge (Shulman, 1986).

One central focus of the coursework in teacher preparation is that teachers learn how to create challenging curriculum and how to develop and evaluate local performance assessments that engage students in research and inquiry on a regular basis (Laukkanen, 2008; Buchberger & Buchberger, 2004). The preparation also emphasizes learning how to teach students who learn in different ways, teaching diverse learners, including those with special needs. It includes substantial emphasis on "multiculturality" and the "prevention of learning difficulties and exclusion," in courses like, "Facing Specificity and Multiplicity: Education for Diversities" and "Cultural Diversity in Schools" along with a course on "Education and Social Justice" as well as on the understanding of learning, assessment, and curriculum development (Buchberger & Buchberger, 2004, p. 6).

Clinical preparation: The "teacher training school" tradition. While preparing to become a teacher requires extensive coursework, Finnish teacher preparation also includes substantial clinical requirements intended to provide lengthy opportunities to learn in real clinical practice. During their preservice period, Finnish elementary school teachers have three periods of clinical experience. Two of these three periods are always at "teacher training schools" associated with the University's teacher education program. All eight universities throughout Finland have at least one teacher training school associated with them—there are eleven teacher training schools in total.

The teacher training school is an important and unique feature of Finnish teacher education. These schools are owned by the universities and administrated by the faculties where teacher education is located in that university. Teacher training schools are public schools that are subject to national curriculum and teaching requirements just like any other municipal school near them. However, teacher training schools have been particularly designed pedagogically and often also architecturally to support both pupils and teacher-students in their learning. Teachers in these schools are required to hold a strong professional record of teaching and advanced studies in educational sciences. As university units, teacher training schools are funded by universities. The Ministry of Education and Culture has a separate budget line for all teacher training schools that it allocates to the universities as part of annual agreement between the universities and the Ministry (but the funding for the training schools is roughly equivalent to regular public schools, with the exception of extra money for supervision of student-teachers).[8] Teacher training schools that were initiated by the universities to offer students safe and structured environments to practice teaching have been a part of teacher education for almost a century in Finland (Paksuniemi, 2009; see also Uusiautti & Määttä, 2013). The Viikki training school, for instance, one of the two teacher training schools associated with the University of Helsinki, has been in existence as a training school since 1934 (Toom, personal communication).

The current site for Viikki, for example, was built in 2003 with special features that would support learning about teaching (see Figure 6). The school is an ordinary school in that it serves students who live in the neighborhood. It is a comprehensive school, serving children in grades 1–9. An associated kindergarten abuts the main building, so that children can also attend as 5 and 6 year olds. However, the main purpose of the school is also to support the learning of prospective teachers: as Principal (for Grades 1–9), Kimmo Koskinen[9] explains, the school is constantly hosting student-teachers: "We have student teachers here all the time. The term starts in August, in the middle of August, and it ends here in the beginning of June. There [are] only two weeks in August and a couple of weeks in May where we don't have student teachers." Koskinen estimated that at any one time, the school typically has between 30–36 student-teachers placed in various classrooms throughout the grades.

Among the special features of the school are a suite of rooms for student-teachers, including a room with tables for meetings among student-teachers, lockers and bookcases for materials and resources, and a coatroom and lunch space. An entire room, equipped with the latest technology, designed for meetings between student-teachers and practice teachers (see Figure 7), underscores the importance that is placed not only upon learning to teach but upon analyzing teaching. During

Figure 6   Viikki Teacher Training School

Figure 7   Student-Teacher Suites

a recent visit, researchers observed student-teachers meeting with their practice teachers in the room to debrief a lesson plan and to talk about next steps. This attention to the cycle of planning, action, and reflection / evaluation is modeled throughout the teacher education, demonstrating what full-time teachers do in planning for their own students. Graduates are expected to eventually engage in similar kinds of research and inquiry in their own work as teachers. These meeting sessions underscore the notion that learning in practice does not happen "on its own" without opportunities for teachers to analyze their experiences, relate experiences to research, and engage in metacognitive reflection. In some ways, it models what the entire system is intended to undergo: a process of continual reflection, evaluation, and problem solving, at the level of the classroom, school, municipality, and nation.

For a deeper look at the Finnish teacher training schools, this video of the Viikki training school illustrates some key principles and practices (Link 5).

Teacher training school teachers: Elite, highly educated teachers to prepare new teachers, who function as a "bridge between theory and practice." Teacher training school teachers are also especially selected to teach in the training schools; they typically have more experience as teachers and many of them are actively involved in traditional academic research in education. While the qualifications to work at a teacher training school are technically not particularly stringent (one has to have worked for two years as a teacher); the norm and expectation is that teacher training teachers are highly accomplished, experienced teachers who are actively engaged in research.[10] Sirkku Myllyntausta, a teacher training school teacher explained that while the stated requirements seem minimal, "in practice it is . . . quite hard to get in, . . . you have to have very deep studies or large studies.... I got this job because I had very many different studies." She noted that in fact, "Nowadays it is so hard to come in that most of our newcomers have their doctoral degrees. The requirements on paper are not so very high, but in practice it seems to be that it is harder and harder to get in." She herself is qualified to teach math at the lower secondary level, as well as to teach preschool pupils— along with certification to teach primary level children.

All three of the teachers at the Viikki Teacher Training School interviewed for this case either had Ph.Ds or were working on them or were involved with multiple research projects. One teacher we spoke with, Anni Loukomies (Figure 8), currently teaching fifth grade at the Viikki Teacher Training School, for instance, was prepared as a CLASS teacher, or, primary school teacher, with the accompanying master's degree and bachelor's in psychology. Yet Anni has earned two additional bachelor's

Figure 8   Anni Loukomies

degrees, one in the teaching of mathematics and the other in the teaching of physics, each of which took two years to complete. Thus she is qualified to teach math and physics at the lower secondary level—although reflective of the investment in early education, she was choosing to teach at the primary level. Therefore, effectively, Anni has substantially more years of teacher education than the five required for primary school teaching, and just last year she completed her Ph.D. Prior to joining the faculty at Viikki, Anni had been teaching for 12 years at a regular primary school.

Sari Muhonen (Figure 9), a third grade teacher and music teacher at the school, has both her master's and bachelor's degrees in Class teacher education, as well as a "licensiate" degree—in other words, she has completed all but the Ph.D. thesis for her doctorate. Sari, like the

Figure 9   Sari Muhonen

other teachers at Viikki, is deeply involved in multiple research projects, including some regarding the new curriculum renewal process.

Sirkku Myllyntausta (Figure 10), another teacher training teacher, is involved in three research projects: an international project on math pedagogy in 12 different countries; a study with the research group of the University of Eastern Finland on Design Oriented Pedagogy regarding certain methods of teacher training—teaching with the University of Eastern Finland; and she just published a book of creative writing with a colleague. She has also been writing textbooks on religion for third, fourth, and fifth graders, along with a group of four other teachers. Sirkku has been teaching at Viikki for 26 years (Link 6). She explained that working at a teacher training school had in fact been a kind of

Figure 10   Sirkku Myllyntausta

dream for her in part due to the strong teaching happening there and the atmosphere of intellectual work that she experienced herself as a student-teacher in a teacher training school:

> When I was young and I was studying to be a class teacher, I was practicing in the teacher training school in Hämeenlinna, so already then I enjoyed the teaching and I enjoyed the atmosphere of the teacher training school, and I admired the class teacher in my class. I remember that already then I had this dream if it could ever be possible, I would like to be a teacher training school teacher.

Sirkku described clearly the benefits of being a teacher training school teacher as a combination of the value of sharing professional expertise; staying updated with new educational research; being challenged intellectually; and constantly learning:

I think the main thing is that after having this long experience as a teacher and having this very deep interest in teaching and interacting with pupils, I feel it is very meaningful to share all of that, and also my occupational skills. In addition, I enjoy discussions with students. I also feel that as a training school teacher it is crucially important to be aware of the latest research in education and the up-to-date teaching methods to be able to apply them in a class with students, and to reflect upon your methods. And you know it kind of keeps me going and in time. It is so fascinating to have this daily cooperation with the students because of the way they challenge me, and my occupational skills.

Anni Loukomies also noted the value and benefits of working in such a school dedicated to the learning of teaching, but that maintained the opportunity to continue to teach young pupils: " it's a really nice combination of supporting the future teachers, supporting the student teachers—and it's kind of a work of a university teacher from that point of view. But still there's a part of that kind of basic work so that you really can work also with the pupils."

Anni described the orientation she takes towards working with student teachers is that her role is to function as a kind of "bridge" between theory and practice, to help student-teachers learn about the relevance of theory to real classroom practice—which also underlies the emphasis of the entire teacher preparation experience upon educational research and theory. She noted that often the student-teachers come thinking that real practice is somehow divorced from theory: "Many student teachers that come here, they see this theoretical studies and the practice here at school, they see them completely distant and completely different from each other. And they are like, '*Okay, now we are going to get rid of the theory and now we're starting to really practice.*' But, she explained that her work was to help students see the relationships between research and classroom practice:

As supervisors, we try to find out like a relevant way of saying to them that . . . now this is the place where you should be combining what you have been studying beforehand. [So] through which concepts you should be reflecting what you are doing here? And what are the phenomena that you meet here? And that's—if I had to describe my position in two words, I would say that I'm a bridge between theory and practice. And I have to somehow distribute that idea to the student teachers and be an example of how to reflect the issues from the practical live with theoretical terms.

Clinical experiences. The first set of experiences occurs during student-teachers' very first year of teacher preparation; the first year of their five

Table 1   Clinical Requirements for Class
Teacher Education Program, University of Helsinki

Practice Period	Length	Activity	Location
First Year	Several days	Observing class; charting social interactions in a class; writing case study of a student; interviewing pupils	Teacher training school
First Year	3 weeks	18 lessons teaching Finnish and drama (9 lessons each in pairs for total of 18 lessons)	Teacher training school
Third Year	7 weeks	50 lessons teaching all subjects (50 lessons taught in pairs in math; science; history; gym; music)	Teacher training school
Fifth Year	7–8 weeks	Responsible for curriculum and teaching students all day	"Field school" or teacher training school

year program. It includes a few days of observations, tied to a set of specific assignments, as well as a longer three-week period of practice teaching (see Table 1). These experiences and the first placement are always at one of the two practice schools; for primary school or CLASS teacher education in Helsinki, this always takes place at Viikki because the other training school does not have a place for primary school teachers—it is a secondary level school. The initial focus of the few days during the first year is to chart children's social interactions and friendships, and to begin to understand the social community of the classroom. Students also write a case study that focuses upon a child in that classroom, also tied to particular classes they take at the university.

Later that first year, pairs of student-teachers return to the *same* classroom, where they charted the social interactions—because they are learning who their students are—and spend three weeks focusing upon the teaching of Finnish (they must teach at least 10 hours) and drama, because at this point in their first year they have only completed their coursework in the methods of teaching Finnish and drama. The students teach in a pair, for a total of 18 lessons (9 lessons each), planning together and acting as co-teachers in one another's lessons. They also develop at least one short integrated project based on themes in Finnish and drama.

The second placement, which is six weeks (one planning week and 5 teaching weeks; 10 lessons a week for the pairs), occurs during the

student-teachers' third year, and requires that the candidates have practice teaching all the remaining subjects (math, science, history, as well as
music and gym and arts, textile and technical work). They must complete
50 lessons in pairs—25 lessons each, with each student responsible for
25 lessons. They plan and enact all 50 lessons together, and each acts as
a co-teacher in the other's lessons. So, together the students write all 50
lessons, planning together, writing the sequence and the broader goals.
Then they divide the lessons in half and teach every week so that each
week both of them are responsible for half of the weeks' 10 lessons. The
other teacher always acts as a co-teacher, observing, helping with struggling students, pitching in as needed.

This placement is always at one of the two teacher training schools.
The master teacher—or practice teacher—is always there, observing as
well. Student-teachers receive feedback every day; they also participate
in co-planning activities with their practice teachers and partner from
their teacher education program. Anni Loukomies, the fifth grade Viikki
practice school teacher, describes what typically happens when student
teachers practice in her room:

> When the student teachers are teaching, … I will be sitting in the class-
> room and I have the lesson plan. They have a broader sequence plan
> and then they have more detailed lesson plan, like what are the aims
> for a certain activity?… How are they going to implement that plan
> and how are they going to be evaluating their students' activities? And
> usually, we check the lesson plan beforehand and they will be briefly
> telling me what are the main points in the plan, and then afterwards,
> we sit down … and discuss the lesson. I try to lead those discussions so
> that if there has been something problematic that needs to be changed
> for the next time, this issue comes from the student teachers them-
> selves. Usually they are kind of nicely reflecting their own teachings, so
> usually they notice the problematic aspects themselves.

The final placement, during the fourth or fifth year, can occur at the
teacher training school, or at a "field school," which is a little more like a
regular school but one that is also intended to prepare teachers. During the
final placement, student-teachers are fully responsible for teaching students
for a period of five weeks. During this time, one candidate teaches for a
week, while the other observes and helps out. They spend the first week of
the five planning together and observing; the second week teaching all of
the lessons together in a pair. The third week one teaches while the other
is co-teaching and assisting; the fourth week they switch roles and the last
and fifth week they teach again together. So each one has an opportunity
to teach students during the entire day—however, by this time they have

had four and a half years of preparation, have developed curriculum, have observed in classrooms, have practiced teaching in a supportive environment, and have been gradually introduced into the teaching profession.

The University of Helsinki maintains a regular field school network that consists of regular schools around the metropolitan area. These schools (principals and teachers) have applied to the network, and have been accepted. They are required to participate in supervision coursework and training that is offered by the department of teacher education, in order to ensure the nature of supervision of student-teachers who practice at the field schools.

An emphasis upon research and analysis of teaching. Another key unique feature of teacher education in Finland is the emphasis of teacher education upon research, inquiry, and analysis of teaching and learning—which includes the study of research methods and a master's degree thesis. These competencies are considered central to the development of professional teachers. This means that all courses integrate educational research, and for primary teachers, educational science is their major and the focus of their five years (Kansanen, 2007; Krokfors, 2007; Toom et al., 2010). The idea behind this approach is that teachers are autonomous professionals who are reflective and systematic in their practice, and are prepared to use a research-based approach in their work (Hökkä & Eteläpelto, 2014). This investment in preparing teachers means that Finnish teachers develop a sense of agency, paired with a considerably strong and rich knowledge base of research and practice, in turn contributing to the overall capacity of the teaching profession as a whole to analyze, to reflect, to practice research-based teaching and to feel responsible and valued as independent practitioners of their work. Furthermore, the kinds of research that teachers engage in are not those tied to student test scores, but rather, represent in-depth examinations of student behavior, work, and thinking.

For primary level teachers—who have had to demonstrate their ability to make sense of educational research in the VAKAVA, in their entry requirements into the program—this means that they must take courses in research methods and inquiry, including a course in qualitative methods and one in quantitative methods, and must also write both a bachelor's and a master's thesis (for a total of 70 ECTS credits). The preparation in research methods and inquiry around pedagogical questions and issues also captures the understanding that the study of children, one's discipline, and teaching practices are integral to the work of teaching. The bachelor's thesis might treat any topic that is of interest to the student. However, the master's thesis typically takes up a topic related to teaching—and is quite closely tied to schools and classrooms.

The program offers considerable support for these master's level theses: faculty sponsor and supervise small research groups of three to seven students who are investigating issues close to the interests and expertise of faculty. For instance, Anu Laine, the director of the CLASS teacher education programs, runs the research meeting for students who are interested in studying topics related to the teaching and learning of mathematics. As she explained, "my latest master theses were about pupil assessment in mathematics. . . . And one was researching [high] achieving children. She followed them from third to sixth grade . . . to see what affects that you are good at mathematics in sixth grade. Can you see it in third grade or not? So it was really interesting." She sees the value of learning to do research as informing how prospective teachers see their work as teachers: "We want them to be researchers, as teachers and researchers, so they understand that they are combined, so that they are not separated, but they are combined and it's useful to research your own work and think what you are doing." (Link 7)

One particularly interesting feature of primary school teachers in Finland is that those who have earned a master's degree (in other words, all primary teachers except those teaching kindergarten) are not only qualified and have ready access to earn a doctoral degree, but some of them choose to pursue such studies (Sahlberg, 2015). Like the teacher training school teachers we spoke with, many choose to do so, often while continuing to teach, and produce dissertations that focus upon some aspect of teaching and learning. Dissertations completed by these candidates focus upon a range of topics: for instance, Anni Loukomies's Ph.D. thesis focused upon students' motivation in science. Of course, doctoral studies are also available for those teaching lower and upper secondary.

Subject Teacher Education

Teachers preparing to teach at the secondary level are similarly required to undergo extensive preparation for teaching. In comparison to primary teachers, however, secondary level teachers are not required to take the VAKAVA and they do not necessarily need to decide upon teacher preparation before entering the university. They still must complete extensive coursework in their subject areas (at least 60 ECTS, which is the equivalent of one full academic year), and take considerable pedagogical preparation as part of their master's degree preparation for teaching (again, one full academic year, or the equivalent of 60 ECTS credits) [see Figure 11]. Upon deciding to apply for teacher education, applicants are selected based upon interviews and grades in their subject areas at the

Figure 11   Curriculum of Subject Teacher Education Programs

HELSINGIN YLIOPISTO
HELSINGFORS UNIVERSITET
UNIVERSITY OF HELSINKI

Structure of pedagogical studies for teachers
60 ECTS credits

BACHELOR'S LEVEL 25 ECTS credits	MASTER'S LEVEL 35 ECTS credits
1st period 18 ECTS credits	**3rd period** 17 ECTS credits
Psychology of development and learning (4 cr)	Social, historical, and philosophical foundations of education (5 cr)
Special education (4 cr)	Evaluation and development of teaching (7 cr)
Introduction to subject teaching (10 cr)	Applied practice (5 cr)
2nd period 7 + 6 ECTS credits	**4th period** 12 ECTS credits
Basic practice in Teacher Training School (7 cr)	Teacher as a researcher -seminar Part 2: Pedagogical thesis (4 cr)
────────────────────────────	Master's level practice in Teacher Training School (8 cr)
Master's level studies in 2nd period	
Teacher as a researcher -seminar Part 1: Research and methods (6 cr)	

1 ECTS credit = 27 hours of work

Department of Applied Sciences of Education
Faculty of Behavioural Sciences

university. There are two main pathways to becoming a subject teacher: candidates can complete a master's degree in an academic program with one major subject (like Finnish or mathematics) and one or two minor subjects (drama, music). Candidates then apply to the Department of Teacher Education for the subject teacher education program. The other option is for a prospective teacher to apply directly to subject teacher education—in this case candidates take two years of subject area studies and then begin pedagogical studies. In both pathways candidates follow the same curricular content, and the only difference is the timing of coursework.

Some recent evidence suggests that it is becoming harder to recruit students in math, physics, chemistry, and some foreign languages (Niemi et al., 2012), and the university secondary teacher education program has had to shift from what they term an "elimination approach" to a "recruitment approach" in those areas. Recent interviews with secondary teacher education faculty at Helsinki, for instance, suggests that their acceptance rates vary from a low of 10% in easy to staff fields to a high of 40% for some candidates in hard-to-recruit areas (Jenset, Klette, & Hammerness, 2013).

The emphasis upon research-based teaching also is reflected in the preparation of secondary level teachers: prospective secondary level teachers must take courses in research methods and must also complete a master's level thesis. In addition, both secondary and primary student-teachers also take a course on how to write about research, which further underscores the emphasis upon not only having a research disposition, but upon sharing one's findings and knowledge with an audience.

Who teaches teachers? Anu Laine, the director of the primary teacher education program, summed up the value placed upon classroom teaching even within the faculty in teacher education by noting, "We are all teachers first." Faculty in the Department of Teacher Education have all had experience as classroom teachers; they have also had considerable experience preparing teachers.

Laine explained that when she talks about her work to others, she feels respected and valued. She feels that Finnish people treat her and her work as important, noting that she feels that they believe: *"She's working at the university, she [has a] Ph.D. She must be very clever.'* I think that they think like that .... It's really valued to be a doctor and a lawyer, but it's also valued to be a good teacher and it's really highly valued in our society to become a teacher."

Studies of the organizational context of teacher education faculty also confirm that teacher educators enjoy a strong sense of agency in terms of making choices about their work, coupled with a clear identity as teacher educators (Hökkä & Eteläpelto, 2014). Interestingly, however, these studies also revealed that teacher educators in Finland did not necessarily view themselves as researchers—a somewhat surprising finding given the very strong emphasis upon research in Finnish teacher education. Rather, teacher educators seem to identify strongly as teachers, but much less strongly as researchers (Hökkä & Eteläpelto, 2014). It may be that in their blended teaching and research roles, school-based educators are more likely to emphasize their research roles, while university-based educators are more likely to want to underscore that they identify with teachers.

Similarly, within the University of Helsinki, the Institute of Behavioral Sciences (where the Department of Teacher Education is housed) is considered valuable and enjoys an equally high status in relationship to other schools within the university. Education faculty we interviewed did not feel that the Department of Teacher Education was viewed with any less high regard than the school of medicine or law, for example. Anu Laine pointed out that the considerable competition for spots in the primary teacher education program, of course, helped solidify the strong reputation of the school of education. Yet it is important to recognize that while the number of students who hope to attend the school may bolster the reputation of the school of education, there is a university-wide focus and appreciation for teaching, not only at the primary and secondary level, but also at the level of university faculty.

The Teachers' Academy at the University of Helsinki

Recently, the University of Helsinki began an effort to recognize outstanding teaching at the faculty level, by initiating a community called the *Teachers' Academy* (see Shulman, 2000, for a description of the scholarship of teaching). In order to join this community, university professors, researchers, and other teaching staff at the university who have made teaching a high priority of their work and who are recognized by students and other faculty as being excellent teachers, may apply. Acceptance bestows upon faculty an honorarium and the status of a Member of the Teaching Academy. The university website makes clear that the establishment of the Teaching Academy reflects "an indication of the value the university community places on the quality of teaching" (University of Helsinki, 2014, Teachers' Academy website).

In this next section we demonstrate how the focus upon developing quality teaching plays out in classrooms and schools in Finland, once candidates graduate from their preservice teacher education.

After Graduation: Supports for Quality Teaching in Schools

As graduates of teacher preparation move into their full-time teaching positions, the emphasis upon preparation, equity, research, collaboration, and scholarship plays out such that teachers in schools maintain a strong sense of professional ethic, a commitment to equity, a feeling of responsibility for student learning, and a sense of autonomy and purpose. In light of these policies aimed at promoting equity, continuing professional development, teaching as a profession, and the commitment of the overall teaching workforce—the result is a continued high quality teaching corps throughout the system. In this section, we elaborate the policies and practices that continue to support, promote, and foster quality teaching in Finland.

In this section, we highlight three key themes. First, we reveal the ways that teachers' work reflects the interlocking and aligned policies around equity and responsibility, differentiation, and work with diverse learners—the elements of which are seeded in preservice training—by drawing on examples of practice in schools. Next, we demonstrate the ways in which a research and inquiry orientation—also treated extensively in initial teacher education—plays out in real schools. Finally, we demonstrate the ways in which teachers take responsibility for professional growth and assessment, and for children's learning in ways that move beyond standardized assessments, test-based outcomes, or countrywide skills tests. We also share how teachers themselves are assessed—and detail some of the qualitative nature of the ways teachers receive feedback as well as identify areas needing improvement.

The Role of the Teacher in Finnish Schools

Teachers' research and inquiry orientation in practice: Innovation at Koulumestari and Poikkilaakso

How does the emphasis upon research and inquiry—that is so intentionally seeded in initial teacher education—play out in real teachers' classrooms? As part of our case study research, we interviewed teachers at several local schools in Helsinki about the ways they used (or did not use) a research orientation in their teaching. The approach teachers described in their teaching reflected a sense of their work as innovative and experimental. The process they used to develop materials, curriculum, and even the structures of student groupings involved explicit testing of "hypotheses" and the gathering of data on such approaches, sharing of results and changes in practice.

For instance, the Koulumestari school in Espoo (a city just outside of Helsinki), is a school of almost 350 students from first through sixth grade which has been specifically designed to serve students with special needs (approximately 20% of the children in the school). It also has a special focus upon the integration of new technology into learning. The work of the teachers in the school reflects a strong orientation towards experimentation, hypothesis testing, and sharing of results with colleagues. The staff of the school hosts what they call a "pedagogical café" four times a year, during their regular monthly staff meetings (Hatch & Hammerness, 2014a). At these times, the teachers share with one another what they are doing with their students, particularly pilot experiments using different technologies.

One outcome of these opportunities has been curriculum that involves students in testing the use of mobile phones in school for the purposes of tracking school assignments; another has been the development of a curriculum that involves children in designing a new technology (for instance, one child developed a rain boot that didn't sink into the ground); a third has been the involvement of children in teaching adults at the school about new technologies.

Another outcome—at the structural level of the school—has been the development of "combined classes" in several grades in which two teachers with classes of about 20 students and one teacher with a class of about 10 special education students all work together to share the teaching for all of the roughly 45–50 students. These combined classes grew out of an initial experiment when several teachers at one grade level decided to try combining their classes; as other teachers learned how it was working, it spread to other levels and groups of teachers.

Similarly, in the Poikkilaakso school, co-teaching and collaboration were considered guiding principles for the school as an organization. The teachers with whom we spoke described co-teaching as well as the creation of opportunities for students to learn across grades and group-ings. Principal Marja Riitta Rautaparta described the organization of teachers' work at the school:

> We don't actually call it "co-teaching" anymore because we see it as something much more deeper. Two teachers have common students, and together they are responsible for planning instruction for, teaching and evaluation of approximately 50 students. Furthermore, two teachers are paired with another two teachers, and together these four teachers and 100 students form a so-called basic unit in our school.

The school was designed so that two study groups existed for grades 1–2 and 3–6, along with some opportunities for grades 2–3 and 4–5 together, so that the content of the subjects they were taught were not considered as "tied" to grade levels. According to one of the Poikkilaakso teachers, Kirsi-Maria Ketola, the groups are formed according to age as it is rather natural criteria for putting children together and form a "home group." In practice, students learn contents from the whole study ensemble all the time (i.e., grades 1–2 or 3–6), but in principle it is even more possible for the students to proceed at their own pace. The result is that students can learn subject matter topics, content and issues that are typically associated with grade 3 all the way to grade 6 during the same school day. Indeed, the school has developed curriculum that reflect a range of grades and the content is considered as tied more broadly to grades 1–2 or 3–6, rather than to specific grades and ages.

Teachers we interviewed from Poikkilaakso reported that working in pairs meant that they were constantly engaging in a kind of "inquiry" in their teaching and daily work as they were consistently testing pedagogical hypotheses in practice to see what was (and was not) effective for their students, and as they had substantial opportunities to observe, analyze, and give feedback to their teacher pairs. The idea of cooperation in Poikkilaakso involves students too. They have formed student work groups that have teachers mentoring them; these groups plan school events or educate other students and teachers about issues, such as recycling. Thus, students have responsibilities as members of the school community and are encouraged to work for the betterment of the community.

Quality Teaching for All

One important feature of Finnish policy around equity is that children with special needs are understood very broadly in Finland, as opposed to the United States. First, Finnish education policy intentionally reflects an inclusive approach to children with special needs—in contrast to a more traditional approach which focuses upon the "disabilities" of children who must fit into the institutions who provide for them. Scholars of inclusive education, however, have argued that creating designations like "special education" and "general education" perpetuate these conceptions and contribute to the persistence of inequities (Graham & Jahnukainan, 2011).

The development of the comprehensive school in Finland was intended to keep *every* student in the same school system, and one approach that emerged was a practice of "part-time special education" for those students in need (Graham & Jahnukainen, 2011), which has been the strategy in use since the 1980's in Finland. But what is most important about this strategy and the way it is framed is *who* is considered a student with special needs, and what seems remarkable is the very inclusiveness and broadness of this conceptualization. In clear contrast to a "wait to fail" approach, the way this policy is enacted means that a child with special needs is seen as *any* child who needs additional support or help— whether the child has particular and long-term challenges that might fit particular categories of OECD special needs definitions, or whether the child happens to be struggling at the moment with a particular concept, like multiplication, or understanding similes. This conception frames children with special needs as fitting within a broad and naturally occur- ring *continuum of variation* rather than designating children with special needs as having *disabilities*. Thus, the development of children's abilities is supported, rather than labeled and categorized.

Around 30% of Finnish students in grades 1–9 receive some form of special support, "which is undoubtedly some kind of unofficial world record" (Graham & Jahnukainen, 2011; see also Statistics Finland, 2014a). But what is particularly and equally remarkable is that the num- ber of students who are identified as needing special support (or, in US terms, children with special needs) appears to be *lower* in secondary schools. One explanation offered by special education scholars Graham and Jahnukainen is that studies have suggested that the focus of Finnish special education is in the early grades, intended to be a kind of preven- tative measure. It seems possible that the work of identifying, assessing, and supporting children with a range of needs pays off in later years of schooling. This seems especially important given the high retention rates of children in Finnish schools—in 2007, senior year students were retained at a level of 89% (Statistics Finland, 2007).

Within the last three years (since 2011), there have been additional changes to the system in the form of additional amendments to the BEA and the National Core Curriculum (2004) for pre-primary and basic education regarding supporting children with special needs. Since then the Finns have been emphasizing support-based conceptualizations, such as "Support for learning and schooling" instead of terms that are medi- cal or diagnostic and lead to labeling (Basic Education Act 628/1998; see also National Core Curricula http://www.oph.fi/english/curricula_ and_qualifications/basic_education). These amendments to the BEA and NCC, which move Finland from a two-tiered to a three-tiered system of supports for children, mean that the range of supports now offered is even broader (Thuneberg et al., 2013, 2014). The new three-tiered system conceptualizes supports for children's learning as being offered at three levels of increasing intensity and support. The first tier consists of *good quality education* which may include differentiated learning, flexible groupings, co-teaching; the second—and newly added—tier consists of more *intensified support* in the form of a learning plan; and the third tier consists of *special support* in the form of an individual education plan (Thuneberg et al., 2013). Only the third tier requires an official decision. In practice, there are a set of interlocking strategies that help support the enactment of these three tiers (and reflect a focus upon teaching for equity) which range from a conceptualization of the teacher as the key player in promoting equity; the use of an additional teacher in the classroom (the "special teacher"); and a team approach to addressing learning differences.[11]

One of the front line strategies of Finnish policy around equity is the conceptualization of the teacher as a key player in promoting support for all students' learning. Teachers are considered critical to ensuring that all students have access to the same resources and support—and, if necessary, additional and targeted individually designed support to enable them to learn and grow. Identifying children who may be falling behind, or even having some minor challenges, or who may struggle with particular concepts in mathematics or with reading comprehension as well as children with more long-term challenges and special needs—all of these are considered the purview of the teacher, but this effort is not left until the formal evaluation and tests are completed, or until annual exams are over. Rather, teachers approach these issues as important to address in the moment—an instantaneous, real-time response to student needs. In the classroom, this means that teachers are consistently rearranging student groups, identifying children who need help, paying special attention to the student who has questions or misunderstands, to the student whose attention lags, as well as if there are more considerable challenges with comprehension, analysis, or understanding. Teachers might meet with children before or after school, during lunch, or during the day. The school day is organized so that these small groups can occur when needed—all this support would be considered general, first tier support for all children.

In addition, a second way this policy is enacted is in two particular teacher positions in Finnish schools, both the "special teacher" and the "part-time special education teachers" (part-time referring to their distributed time in various classrooms throughout the school day—it is a full-time teaching position). Most schools have one or two such "part-time special education teachers" in addition to the regular "class teacher"; the part-time special education teacher might co-teach, or give small group instruction to children who need additional support (mostly at the second, "intensified support" tier). *Part-time special education teachers* have graduated from the special education teacher education program and thus have five years of specific training for this position. Typically, a school might have one or two *part-time special education teachers* who work throughout the school. These teachers most often work at the elementary level with a small group that consists of pupils that are receiving special support; and these pupils often have been officially designated as special education students with IEPs, and receive special support in the small group full-time or part-time. Schools may also have regular classrooms teachers on the other hand, who have been trained first as elementary school teachers but who then go on to take an additional year of study of support for children with special needs; they are designated as *special teachers*. Kimmo Koskinen, the practice-school principal in Helsinki, noted that both of these types of teachers are important in helping children *constantly* in the classroom: "Because in Finland, there is integration .... and inclusion brings many kinds of pupils in the classroom, so the other [teacher] is helping them all the time."

Finally, while teachers take individual responsibility for students' learning and development for a wide range of learners, they also have a more collaborative strategy available for more persistent challenges or to help children whose needs are broader or more lasting. Teachers work together in multidisciplinary teams—consisting of the regular, class teacher, the part-time special education teacher, the school counselor, along with some people outside the schools, such as social workers from health services, representatives from the health and mental health community, or from public housing, if necessary—to try to address any issues that might be beyond the immediate purview of the school itself. Therefore, teachers have at their fingertips a wide array of means and supports to draw upon to help children in need.

This means that Finnish teachers are able to distinguish their work of teaching from the broader social, health, economic issues, and at the same time, they are able to collaboratively address these critical larger issues that can directly impact children's ability to succeed. This public acknowledgment of the intermingling of learning and the broader contexts of children's lives enables teachers to focus upon their work of teaching, but also to carefully draw in other supports that can help round out the web of supports for children and their learning and development. So, for instance, if a Finnish teacher realizes that a child cannot attend school because of chronic health problems:

These are the responsibility of a comprehensive health system. Students with mental health problems or family troubles have the resources of the mental health and social welfare system. As noted earlier, public housing takes care of housing needs, reducing the mobility of students. The ability of multidisciplinary teams to call on the resources of the welfare state as well as the education system comes from a special governance structure: block grants for education, health, and social services are allocated to municipalities, which have responsibilities for a wide array of social programs.

(Graham & Jahnukainen, 2011)

Multiculturalism in Schools

While Finland has had a relatively homogenous population, that is changing. As Heljä Misukka, Director of Educational Policy in Trade Union of Education (OAJ), points out, "Every 10th student" is a student from another country, race, or ethnicity aside from Finland. Immigration has been centered in the biggest cities in Finland as in many other countries around the world. For example, in the Myllypuro primary school (one of our focal schools in this case), a school in Helsinki, approximately 40% of students are first or second-generation immigrants.[12]

Adequately and thoughtfully responding to students who bring knowledge, experiences, and cultures different from those native to Finland have been central to the planning of the Ministry for some time. The new 2016 national curricular framework http://www.oph.fi/english/ education_development/current_reforms/curriculum_reform_2016, for example, includes "multiliteracy" among seven overarching goals (Halinen, 2014). Armi Mikkola, Counselor of Education in Ministry of Education, identified multiculturalism as one of the central future questions for teacher education programs, as well as for teachers already working in the field—and specifically, noted that a growing linguistic awareness was critical for prospective teachers more than ever. As she noted:

> Looking at the future, every teacher needs to—actually already now—realize that she or he is a linguistic model and language teacher [in Finnish for first and second generation students]. Teachers should be able to teach math in way that the mathematical conceptualization becomes understandable as well as possible for every student. This places new demands for teachers' "linguistic awareness."

Indeed, the claim that Finland is a highly homogenous country is no longer applicable to every school, in every Finnish city. Immigration from nations with lower levels of schooling has increased sharply in recent years, and schools are contending with considerable linguistic and cultural diversity. Estimates suggest that new immigrants in Finland speak more than 60 languages (Darling-Hammond, 2010). Despite these shifts, Finland has maintained its equitable achievement. In fact, the city of Helsinki has a policy that is roughly translated as "positive discrimination" which involves targeting areas and specific schools which are identified as lower-status economically, or having other needs (such as considerable numbers of students who speak Finnish as a second language) and providing extra resources. Anu Laine pointed out the difference in the philosophy of support for struggling schools (Link 8):

> In many countries they have testing, and the schools are getting money if they're *good*. While we are not giving any tests... but we can see that those schools have a more challenging situation. So we give them more money. [So in fact] we are doing the opposite [as the other countries.] If they have lower results ... they are getting more money. I think it's really good.

Myllypuro, one of the schools we studied, receives some of this funding and uses it to hire more teachers, to ensure that students who do not come to school speaking Finnish can receive additional support. In Myllypuro, approximately 15% of the students (60 of 420) come to school speaking Russian as their first language. Jaana Piipponen, a class teacher with over 20 years of experience, explained that the funding has enabled her to have a Russian-speaking co-teacher in her class for several hours every week so that they can co-teach in both languages.

Teacher Appraisal in Finnish Schools: A Focus upon Personal Responsibility and Feedback for Growth

In Finland, the work of teachers is not measured using standardized test outcomes.[13] Rather the assessment of teachers is focused upon professional development at the individual level. Teachers are considered valued professionals who are capable, autonomous, and independent, and in fact, fully responsible for their work in the classroom. In general, teachers' work is evaluated by their principals, and often involves a one-on-one private conversation that may focus upon issues like individual growth, participation in professional development, contributions to the school, and personal professional goals.

Much of the appraisal function is integrated into the ongoing work of teachers with their principal and personnel and occurs informally. Indeed, middle school teachers surveyed by TALIS reported that they receive very little formal feedback and few schools have formal teacher appraisal systems. Almost 28% of teachers in Finland teach in a school where the principal reports that teachers are not formally appraised by the principal. Instead, the main form of appraisal comes from face-to-face and often informal dialog with the school leader. Thirty-seven percent of Finnish teachers report that they have never received feedback on their teaching in school (Sahlberg, 2015; see also OECD, 2014a). These findings further suggest that feedback on teaching is conceptualized in Finland in an in-depth, personal, local manner relying heavily upon qualitative and descriptive data. Indeed, it seems to function in a way that is dramatically different from a heavily mandated external accountability system with which many countries are familiar. To those used to a more systemic and accountability-based perspective, feedback on teaching and professional development may not seem to be happening at all. Yet, at least in the places we studied, the culture around feedback and reflection on teaching is, in fact, strong, purposeful, and integrated and intensely focused in Finland. At the same time, the focus is upon "steering"—the guidance and direction of a professional career, rather than "accounting"—an attempt to ensure that teachers are meeting certain specified goals or outcomes (Link 9) (Hatch, 2014).

In the city of Helsinki, however, principals do use a common form to guide the conversation with teachers. This form focuses upon some key features of teaching that are considered important and valuable. The form, however, does not require any standardized data in any form—no student test scores, no value-added data, no quantitative indicators—but rather focuses upon four categories: "personal performance," "versatility," "initiative," and "ability to cooperate." In addition to analysis of teacher's general classroom practice, the versatility of the teacher refers to whether she or he uses or has mastered "good pedagogical skills," can "acknowledge and meet diverse students in different circumstances," and can "acknowledge diverse learning needs." The form (Link 10) asks teachers and principals to consider the degree to which the teacher demonstrates "initiative" (which includes, for instance, "using new and meaningful working methods and practices"; and "active participation in in-service training, [within school]work groups, development initiatives, district workgroups"). As in the prior example, this suggests that the conception of evaluation in Finland relies heavily upon local, personal, qualitative information about a teachers' practice, growth, and professionalism.

Anna Hirvonen, principal of Myllypuro primary school in Helsinki, described her use of the City of Helsinki's teacher evaluation form to guide her work. She rather emphasized the demanding nature of the evaluation and the importance of knowing her teachers well and coming to agreement upon the content. She also acknowledged the challenges of the evaluation and the degree to which even criteria were still open to interpretation:

> I have, every year, a discussion, called Evaluation of Personal Perfor- mance (EPP) with every teacher where I evaluate how [a teacher's] personal objectives have been reached in terms of ability to cooperate, versatility, initiative and performance. The City of Helsinki has given us the criteria and description of every factor, according to which these aspects are looked at, in practice the factors overlap and are open to interpretation. Furthermore, there is a 5-step scale from "Not fully meets the objectives" to "Excellent performance" where to place all these. The situation itself it is very, very, demanding professionally. If I have worked with some teachers for years and seen how they work and what they do in every day's school work, it is easier, but especially with the beginners, it is really demanding. . . . First time when we had EPPs I used the whole time allocated [45 minutes per teacher] for the personal development conversation to go through the EPP form.

Indeed, Hirvonen's description reveals how much the evaluation con- versation relies upon her work as a principal in knowing her teachers, being in their classrooms and observing and being aware of their work with children and colleagues. While this kind of observational knowl- edge is highly demanding, it also means that principals need to be in classrooms, need to know their teachers and students well and deeply, and need to be engaged in "management by walking around." This approach relies on a kind of closely networked school community.

> Every teacher told me how they see that things are going and then I brought out my viewpoints of their work; how they have reached every objective. If we agreed on things it was easy but we did not always and that was rough. . . . Before the first evaluation round [when it was a new thing] I arranged my schedules and was able to go around the school and visit classes while teachers were teaching, and it was not a short visit but I spent time there. And, sure, I see teachers engaged in many different situations in school with students; on the hallways and if we have to together solve out some challenges. In addition, I observe how teachers participate in school life in general, how they bring in their knowledge for the whole school community's use, how they develop themselves, how they participate in develop- ment processes and so on.

Teachers' and pupils' schedules reflect a broadened conception of teaching as including time for planning, assessing, and collaboration; and learning as including time for play

Teachers' schedules in Finland reflect a conception of teaching that moves beyond "teaching as time in front of students in the classroom." Rather, it suggests that teaching also involves time for planning, collaborating, meeting with other teachers to discuss challenges or successes, and other professional work, such as reading and doing research. Data from the Finnish teachers' union reveals that Finnish primary teachers spend approximately 718 hours per year leading classes; lower secondary teachers, 657; and upper-secondary teachers, 647 (Abrams, 2015).

Indeed, amendments to the Basic Education Act in Finland stipulate that one lesson is 60 minutes of which at least 45 minutes must be used for instruction time (Basic Education Act, 1998; Amendments 2010). In most schools in Finland, a regular lesson lasts 45 minutes which then leaves 15 minutes for recess for both students and teachers. Some schools have lessons that last 60 minutes or 75 minutes. In these schools recess time must be extended respectively. This means that in a typical school day there may be up to 90 minutes recess time, including lunch break. Recess is considered necessary, and is seen as an opportunity for all children to go out or play with friends—as well as providing an important break for teachers who often spend that time either in quick consultations in the teachers' lounge with colleagues or preparing for the next class. Indeed, the choice to have children spend time outside and in informal play is supported by considerable research on cognition and learning (Milteer & Ginsburg, 2012).

Collective labor agreement. Another feature of the conditions of teaching in Finland is that the labor agreements for teachers are negotiated collectively, between the Association of Finnish Local and Regional Authorities (Kuntaliitto) and the Trade Union of Education in Finland, upon regular cycles that normally lasts for about three years Almost all teachers are members of the Trade Union of Education—95% of teachers according to a recent report—and the union represents a critical stakeholder and actor in shaping the development and preparation of teachers (Sahlberg, 2015).

Teacher pay and benefits. Upon graduation, new Finnish teachers can expect to make a reasonable salary that is commensurate with other professions. At the same time, the nature of the social democracy in Finland also means that the range of salaries overall is less broad: indeed, teachers' statutory salaries are "almost equal" to those offered to Finnish workers in other valued fields requiring similar levels of preparation (OECD, 2012, 2013b). For instance, in 2008, general practitioners in Finland were paid an average of USD 65,000 (OECD, 2011); and nurses an average of USD 34,000. As of 2010, teachers' salaries were generally in line with those with similar education (see Table 1.2) (OECD, 2012). But for Finns, more important than salaries are such factors as high social prestige, professional autonomy in schools, and the ethos of teaching as a service to society and the public good. Young Finns see teaching as a career on a par with other professions where people work independently and rely on scientific knowledge and skills that they gained through university studies.

In Finland, compensation grows with experience. Salaries are determined by level of schooling at which they teach: teachers make about 7–10% more for mid-career teaching in lower secondary vs. primary schools; and similarly 7–10% increase between lower and upper secondary (OECD, 2014c). By the time they are experienced teachers, they will have increased their salaries by approximately one-third. Top-scale salaries are 58 (lower secondary)–77 (upper secondary) percent higher than starting salaries.

In 2012, the average initial pay for a beginning Finnish teacher in US dollars converted to purchasing power parity was USD 32,000 at the primary level, and USD 35,000 at lower secondary level and USD 37,000 at the upper secondary level, a little higher than the OECD average (OECD, 2014b). Middle career salaries in Finland were USD 40,000, USD 42,500, and USD 46,000 respectively. The (slightly) higher salary for lower and upper secondary teachers is due in part to having a master's degree in a specific subject area as well as to the fact that they teach slightly more hours per week than primary school teachers (see Table 2).

Teachers' Careers: Organic and Local Novice and Professional Development

One of the challenges for the capacity of the teaching force in Finland, however, may well be the horizontal nature of the teaching profession: as one policy document notes, "in terms of promotion, the teaching career in Finland is flat" (NBER, 2012). In Finland, the professional development continuum may in some ways—at least informally—reflect the relative horizontal nature of the teaching career in that there have been few formal accommodations for new teachers and their novice status and rare opportunities for more veteran teachers to explicitly and publicly shift their status in ways that reflect either their mastery of

Table 2   Ratio of Teachers' Salaries to Earnings for
Full-time, Full-year Workers with Tertiary Education Aged 25–64 in 2010

	Primary education	Lower secondary education	Upper secondary education
Australia	0.92	0.92	0.92
Austria	0.58	0.62	0.64
Canada	1.05	1.05	1.05
Denmark	0.87	0.87	1.01
England	0.99	1.09	1.09
Finland	0.89	0.98	1.10
France	0.73	0.79	0.80
Germany	0.88	0.97	1.05
Iceland	0.50	0.50	0.61
Ireland	0.82	0.82	0.82
Israel	0.85	0.87	0.92
Italy	0.57	0.60	0.64
Korea	1.31	1.30	1.30
Netherlands	0.70	0.84	0.84
New Zealand	0.98	1.01	1.03
Norway	0.66	0.66	0.70
Portugal	1.19	1.19	1.19
Scotland	0.95	0.95	0.95
Spain	1.21	1.35	1.38
Sweden	0.79	0.81	0.86
United States	0.67	0.69	0.72
OECD average	0.82	0.85	0.90
EU21 average	0.81	0.85	0.90

Source: OECD, 2012, Education at a Glance

the field and the work. Yet at the same time, the opportunities for professional development are more local and organic, and democratically organized.

Up until recently, both formal induction—in other words, support and professional development targeted at new teachers—and systematic professional development have not been a strong part of the education system in Finland—and in some ways, this may contribute to (or reinforce) a conception of a teacher's career as remaining at a kind of status quo. Opportunities to participate in formal, external continued professional development vary considerably in Finland—as do opportunities for formal induction for new teachers.

Employers, in most cases *municipalities*, have legal responsibility to offer professional development opportunities to teachers and principals. At the same time teachers have moral responsibility to continuously improve their work. For instance, teachers are required by contract to participate in three professional development days a year; it is considered the responsibility of the individual teacher or school principal to determine how to use that time, and even whether there is funding for professional development beyond those three days (Sahlberg, 2015). A recent report suggests that in 2013, more than 80% of teachers participated in some form of professional development (lasting more than three hours) during the past year (Finnish National Board of Education, 2014a). Data from OECD's TALIS survey confirmed that trend: participation of middle school teachers in professional development was approximately 79% among Finnish lower secondary school teachers (the OECD average was 88%) (OECD, 2014a).

In our interviews we found that the number of days per school year spent in professional development varied considerably; some teachers we interviewed estimated that they had spent somewhere between twenty (and some said up to fifty days) in some form of professional development during the prior school year.

The Ministry of Education has been developing strategies that focus in particular upon professional development, in light of a survey in 2007 that had revealed only two thirds of teachers participated in professional development (Piesanen, Kiviniemi, & Valkonen, 2007). Thus, the Ministry of Education set up a working group in 2008 to determine some measures to improve the situation and to consider legislation regarding professional development. The group, which is made up of all major stakeholders in schools (The Trade Union of Education in Finland (OAJ); the student-teachers union (SOOL) as well as teacher educators, all have representatives on this advisory board), was charged with helping advise the Ministry's decision making regarding teachers' professional development. The final results of the working group in 2009 was a decision not to make professional development obligatory. Instead, they established a new *Osaava* (or in English, *capable* or *skillful*) program that would promote teachers' participation in professional development on a voluntary basis. Funding was allocated to this program in the amount of 8–10 million Euros per year from 2010 to 2016. Five strategic aims underlay the program: (1) Promoting equity and leadership in teachers' lifelong learning; (2) Making flexible learning paths a reality in educational institutions; (3) Enhancing the adaption of innovative professional development models; (4) Improving networking and collaboration among educational institutions and professional development providers; and (5) Mainstreaming successful professional development practices.

What stands out from this Osaava program is the emphasis upon developing a more clear and articulated continuum of professional development that would coherently support teachers' learning over the course of their careers: for instance, about 20% of the funding was specifically allocated to support a mentoring program for new teachers (which had been piloted in 2008 and was being developed nationally in 2010); for supporting the use of educational technology in teacher training schools; and for a program of 30 credits for long-term professional development for educational leaders. In addition, the program also was intended to target teachers 55 or older, as well as teachers with nonpermanent status who (research suggested) were not participating as much in professional development.

Jouni Kangasniemi, senior advisor in Division for Adult Education Policies of Ministry of Education, pointed out that "we are in the middle of a critical period" moving away from earlier state funded models of professional development which have not been as successful, and rather, towards a conception of learning networks. He emphasized that the ideas undergirding Osaava reflect a flexible conception of teacher learning as occurring within more natural, local (or national) networks and communities that enable teachers to learn from one another. He noted: "It is essential to understand that we can use the already existing teachers' know-how and knowledge and innovations to develop others, and to see that 'the wisdom' does not exist outside the schools but inside them." Kangasniemi further noted that a second driving idea behind the network was an understanding that teachers would need both formal and clear institutional structures for professional development, as well as support for more informal, loosely coupled professional development opportunities that might be more local, personal, or specific to individuals. As he explains:

> We [at the Ministry of Education] are building a political framework within which we try to support and create certain actions. On the one hand, some of them are more or less straightforward, readily formulated, and in relation to changes in operational environment or legislation, and on the other, building more day-to-day rooted networks around teachers in order to make the network itself gain the ownership of new information and in that preventing the information from disappearing if actors move from one work community to another.

This professional development in Finland is almost solely funded by the government together with employers. It is not common in Finland, as it is in the United States or Canada, that teachers would pay workshops or training courses from their own pockets. Teachers' contribution to their own professional development is most often "in kind," i.e., learning on their own time. Every year, the Finnish Ministry defines a set of areas for focus (somewhere between 5 and 7 areas), and those areas help shape the distribution of funding for the year, for professional development. The funding for professional development altogether equals about 40–60 million euros per year (half of which comes from the Ministry and the other from the municipalities).

The government in Finland has only limited influence on how funding is allocated in municipalities and schools. Schools therefore have considerable flexibility in how they determine their funding allocations, but that also means that these experiences for teachers may take more or less of a major role in what schools choose to support. During times of economic stress (as is the case now) professional development may be among those aspects of school support that gets cut. Typically professional development is contracted out to service providers such as universities (who have on-site training centers) or private companies who offer opportunities to study practice; to focus upon particular issues such as first and second-generation children in schools; the use of technology in classrooms; and school leadership. Awarding of the contracts is competitively determined and is typically given to professional development and further education centers owned by universities.

Policymakers in Finland also make clear that when a major change is made in the education system, they then work to offer accompanying professional development for teachers. For instance, Jussi Pihkala, Counselor of Education in Ministry of Education, noted that teachers were offered in-service training in relationship to the recent Special Education Reform (the changes, the amendments, made in the Basic Education Act in 2010, which became obligatory in 2011):

> When reforming something there is a resource for in-service training included. For example, the renewal of our support system for students [i.e. the movement from 2-tiered to current 3-tiered model]; there was a lot of funding allocated to help the educational organizers to work with it, to offer professional development for their educational personnel, so, to "put it in action," and the in-service training that is coordinated by the FNBA is ongoing until 2015.

On the other hand, the culture around participation in professional development reflects a quite different conception that emphasizes the local, organic nature of teachers' professional learning in schools in forms that are more democratically organized. So there are factors in Finland that may influence when teachers choose not to participate in more formal external professional development. The state does not currently cover the payment of a substitute teacher who would take over a teachers' classroom during professional development—this is the responsibility of the school or municipality, which must allocate the money for different local services. The policy around formal professional development varies around Finland. For instance, the City of Helsinki's Education Department offers programming that is free of charge for the schools so that schools may use any additional money for some other purposes, i.e., buying new books or other materials. In comparison, the city of Kotka does not organize professional development, so teachers mostly participate in professional development that is organized by the National Board, which is free. The city compensates expenses such as travel and hiring a substitute teacher.

Furthermore, some teachers describe a conflict between taking time for more formal professional development that is external to the school, with their feelings of responsibility for their students. For instance, Leea Pekkanen, class teacher with five years' teaching experience in Myllypuro school, noted that she sees that in principle her primary task is to teach and be with her students. So while she has participated in some of the more formal and external professional development opportunities, she has been forced (due to her commitment to students) to be very selective. Similarly, Jouni Partanen, a subject teacher in Langinkoski lower secondary school in Kotka, explained the dilemma in terms of the disruption that leaving his classroom would require:

> A lot of opportunities are offered to participate in professional development but there is also the question of using your time; if you decide to participate you have to prepare the lessons that are kept while you are away anyway. And even if the teacher substituting you is good it still distracts the overall plan you have made so far.

Jaana Puupponen described in detail her responsibility to build and strengthen the overall trust within her student group and not to leave them for a "stranger" as that violates the trust building process which she sees being at its crucial point. In some ways the teaching culture that promotes strong individual responsibility, autonomy, and focus upon students may, in fact paradoxically, make it more difficult for teachers to choose to participate in formal, external professional development. On the other hand, it makes it more reasonable and appropriate to offer opportunities to grow and learn within one's local school context.

The conception of and organization of opportunities for professional learning and teacher development in Finland are different from than what is typically framed as "professional development"—meaning participation in formal, external workshops or programs that are developed and implemented by educators outside a school in hierarchically organized forms. In our interviews, principals repeatedly described both formal and informal opportunities for dialog, feedback, collaboration, and working in professional teams within the schools themselves. For instance, Principal Heidi Honkanen in Langinskoski lower secondary school in Kotka (a mid-size city about 130 km from Helsinki to East in Southern Finland) emphasized the importance of constant professional dialog and weekly teacher meetings as efficient ways to share new ideas, knowledge, and give peer support to and learn from colleagues. She sees these meetings as an important form of professional development as it is strongly tied to everyday school life and enables handling issues when they still are acute. She also noted that these meetings are also a good way for beginners to learn from more experienced teachers, and vice versa. Indeed, Jouni Partanen, a novice subject teacher (in history and social studies) in Langinkoski, noted that the openness of their school was very important since he felt he could gather new ideas or useful tips for practical solutions from his colleagues even during the short breaks as the teachers share common space. He explained that this kind of in-time local, personal support was crucial for him as a new teacher: "It's very handy since if I have, for example, a practical question concerning how to organize my lessons or so I can just consult some more experienced colleague while we get coffee between the lessons. So, I'm able to get help immediately and not need to wait." Principal Anna Hirvonen in Myllypuro school described organizing "demo-lessons" in their school in which one teacher who has special expertize on some method or some subject teaches a lesson to others, and that enables teachers to enrich their teaching and informs them about new possible ways of doing things. Anna herself has given a demonstration on music as that is her area of expertise. Indeed, our interviews suggest that opportunities for professional learning range from more formal (such as the demo lessons or the "pedagogical cafes") to informal (getting help from more experienced teachers in a shared common space at the school) but are organic and local and democratic—as opposed to professional learning that occurs beyond or external to the school environment.

Up until recently, the formal development and support of new teachers during the induction period has not been as well-articulated in Finland (Sahlberg, 2011). For instance, Finnish law has a probationary period in place for new teachers of six months, but there is no explicit mention of induction support (Laki kunnalllisesta viranhaltijasta 11.4.2003/304). As in many states in the United States, the schools and municipalities are primarily responsible for providing orientation and support for new teachers. Therefore, there have been fewer systematic supports or efforts in place around new teacher induction—and the quality and nature of those supports can vary considerably. As Sahlberg (2015) has noted, some schools, as part of their mission, have adopted advanced procedures and support systems for new staff, whereas other schools merely bid new teachers welcome and show them to their classrooms. However, support for novice teachers in Finland is slowly changing. A growing body of practice and research on this phase of teaching is pointing to some important developments (Heikonen et al., in press). The new network earlier described focusing upon mentoring new teachers was initiated in 2008 as a pilot—the "Osaava Verme" network—is part of the overall nationwide Osaava network described earlier. The network partners with all eight universities which prepare primary and secondary teachers (as well as the vocational teacher education programs which prepare early childhood teachers), and offers support for monthly peer-to-peer meetings for new teachers that are led by more experienced teachers.

Decisions for the Future of Quality Teaching in Finland

Looking towards the future, Finnish educators and policy makers point out some key decisions and developments that continue to support equitable teaching and a strong teacher workforce. For instance, one particular proposal being considered was a National Registry of Teachers—the intention being to make publicly available to parents and school faculty the status of teachers' master's degrees. Such a registry would allow the Ministry and others, for instance, to better track the workforce of teachers and to evaluate future needs in supply and demand of teachers in particular areas. Currently the Finnish National Board of Education sponsors a nationwide survey every third year to gather information about teachers, such as age, participation, mobility, regional distribution, and other key data. That report works as a basis for the Ministry of Education's proposal, made every third or fourth year, regarding teacher preparation and the universities (Armi Mikkola, February 10, 2014). For instance, Jussi Pihkala, Counselor of Education in Ministry of Education, indicated that "special needs education, especially the group of students with the most severe" needs was one area in which Finland could use more support and strong teachers. Supporters of a Qualified Teacher

Registry, such as the OAJ and the Finnish Parents League (Suomen Van-hempainliitto), suggest that it would support such monitoring and data gathering as well as future planning around the teacher workforce.

Currently, efforts to establish an Open Access Qualified Teacher Registry have been slow because an official institution that would oversee it has not yet been identified. While a development plan from the Ministry for Education and Research 2011–2016 advises (Link 11) municipalities and other local educational organizers to create a shared system containing their educational personnel's qualifications (Ministry of Education and Culture, 2012), creating registries at a more local level would not give nationwide consistent information on the issue. In addition, Finnish policy makers have raised concerns that the efforts to maintain such a database might require valuable monetary and personnel resources that could be used more effectively elsewhere.

A second development that reflects the centrality and professionalism of teachers in national discussions and policy is the renewal process of the National Core Curriculum, which takes place approximately every ten years (Vitikka, Krokfors, & Hurmerinta, 2012; see also Halinen, 2014). The process involves numerous "curriculum groups" that develop the guidelines and objectives in each subject and aspect of the core curriculum. Although the process for developing the core curriculum has evolved over time, particularly in the last two renewal cycles there has been extensive involvement of key education stakeholders from the very beginning of the discussions. The Head of Curriculum Development at the Finnish National Board of Education, Irmeli Halinen, emphasizes both the creative and meaningful nature of the curriculum development process: "Elsewhere [in most countries] they talk about 'curriculum implementation' but here it is a creative process. It is truly about planning and thinking about your own work from different perspectives. There have been whole school communities involved: teachers, principals, parents and students...This collective process of reflection and debate characterizes Finnish national core curriculum, and, also, makes it meaningful for teachers."

Indeed, teachers are at the center of these committees, though the committees also include school leaders, municipal administrators, teacher educators, and researchers, among others whom themselves been teachers at some point in time.[14] In past revision cycles, opportunities were made available to give feedback to the draft curriculum before it was formally adopted. The most recent revision has been the most "open" of all (Hatch & Hammerness, 2014b). Surveys have been sent to all the municipalities so that school faculty can share their responses to initial drafts; municipalities and schools have been encouraged to share and discuss the initial proposals with parents and students; and initial drafts of the curriculum have been made available online so that anyone who wants to can provide feedback.

That feedback came from numerous individuals and from more than 200 different organizations representing many aspects of Finnish society. Members of the committees are looking at that feedback as they make revisions. The feedback addressed the broad objectives as well as the specific language used. (For example, the use of the word "tolerance" in an early draft's discussion of diversity and culture was changed because of feedback that it conveyed a limited sense of acceptance, rather than mutual respect and understanding.) In the end, the curriculum groups will make the proposals for the new guidelines and the leaders of the National Board of Education will make the final decision.

Although this open process can be unwieldy, the wide engagement of teachers, leaders, teacher educators, textbook publishers, researchers, parents, students, and others in the process creates social connections that facilitate the sharing of information and knowledge about the changes *long before those changes are actually made* (Hatch & Hammerness, 2014b). Indeed the working committees and feedback process has been going on since about 2012, well before the new core curriculum is scheduled to be formally adopted this year and long before the required development of new local curriculum (based on the national curriculum) in 2016. That means that those who are involved in supporting the work of teachers and students—like teacher educators and textbook publishers—are already getting a sense of where the revisions are heading and what kinds of changes they will need to make so that the whole system is "ready" at the introduction of the new local curriculum.

Because teachers have been so central to this process, as Hannele Cantell, a former teacher and faculty member at the University of Helsinki who teaches in the subject teacher education program points out, they do not express stress or concern about the curricular change—because the teachers have already seen drafts, and read and reviewed multiple versions. "They know what is coming," as she explained. Even with this major policy development, teachers play a central and pervasive role—not only illustrating the ways in which respect and value is afforded to the work of teaching, but also the deliberate decisions to involve those who play a central role in working with learners, in the work of considering the curriculum. Indeed, the curriculum revision is an excellent example of the ways in which policy choices have been deliberately made that put the work of teachers—and the knowledge, expertise, and experience of teachers—at the center of key policy decisions and national efforts involved in education. It also reflects the strong sense of shared vision—a shared sense of purpose—and commitment to education for all that underlies the Finnish approach (Halinen, 2014).

A Case of the "Construction" of Teacher Quality

Our examination of the deliberate and intentional policy work that has taken place in Finland over the past fifty years suggests that this is indeed a case of "constructing" teacher quality. We argue that over a relatively short time period, policy makers, politicians, educators, and teachers have together worked in coherent ways to systematically deliberate and consider, and in turn create and build, the necessary supports, systems, policies leading to a context in which teachers and children can do the hard work of teaching and learning, and ultimately can thrive. The policies have not been rushed or pushed into place, but rather have been developed quite gradually and incrementally (such as policy around children with special needs). Such considered and step-wise implementation may also have resulted in more time and space for teachers and educators (as well as schoolchildren) to respond and adjust to changes.

Furthermore, the policies have often been developed in concert with teachers or by policy makers who themselves have been teachers or have had teacher training. In turn, as Finnish documents emphasize, "The aim of Finnish policy is coherent policy" such that the majority of the specific, individual policy choices and decisions reflect a set of broad beliefs—or vision—about the importance of equity; the centrality of children and their need for time, thinking, play, and choice; and a belief about teaching as professional and worthy of the utmost respect, value, and status. In this case, seven key themes seem to underlie this kind of construction of quality:

- The coherent and alignment of policies for teaching and teacher preparation
- The continued emphasis upon the well-being of children (and their teachers)
- The focus upon teachers' agency and professional responsibility
- An investment in learning to teach in practice with considerable university support
- The conception of professional development as local, organic, and in-time

ᴑ The constant consideration of equity through an emphasis upon *education for all children*

ᴑ The reflection of a developmental perspective on both childhood and teaching

Aligned and Coherent Policies around Teaching and Teacher Preparation

In the work of constructing quality, this case demonstrates how the multiple decisions about the nature, quality, and development of Finnish teachers together reflect an intention to support and sustain a quality teaching workforce that enables equitable learning for all students. The case sheds light on the multiple and embedded ways in which Finnish policy and practical decisions reflect continued attention to considerations about equity and access—values central to the educational system in Finland. These choices play out in decisions regarding the thorough and sustained preparation of teachers in universities; the multiple strategies for selection; the support for professional autonomy and independence; the acknowledgment of the importance of learning in practice; the sustained effort to make equitable teaching available to all pupils; and the development of a system that both supports and values the work of teaching.

In short, this consistency yields a kind of policy coherence that supports the development of a sense of shared focus and a common understanding that can help support teachers and teaching (Hatch & Hammerness, 2014b; Hatch, 2015). This coherence is reinforced by the fact that almost all of those who are involved in education (policy makers, teacher educators, textbook writers) all initially trained as classroom teachers, prepared through teacher education. Teacher educators such as Hannele Cantell were not only on the curriculum committee but were also writing textbooks that reflected the new curriculum (and were also former teachers). Furthermore, the slow and deliberate decision making not only enables and supports multiple perspectives but also allows the time and space necessary for real change. For instance, the gradual efforts to bring children with special needs into the comprehensive schools was managed over a number of years in order to allow educators time to develop approaches and structures that would support them and enable teachers to be successful with all their students. The efforts to redesign the national curricular framework using an open, interactive, cooperative, and gradual process promotes a cycle that allows for critical dialog, enables early identification of solutions to emerging challenges, and builds commitment by all key stakeholders to the goals and the end result.

An Investment in Learning to Teach in Practice Paired with Considerable Theoretical Support

A related key theme that emerges from this case is an investment in learning to teach in practice, in ways that are highly coordinated and integrated with "training schools." The training school tradition—perhaps most central in preparing primary school teachers—reflects an appreciation not only for the importance of learning to teach itself but also for learning to teach in practice. However, the training school tradition does not reflect a conception of learning to teach in unsupported ways. Nor does it imply a belief that learning to teach happens on its own simply because one is working in the field in real classrooms. Rather, learning to teach in training schools puts forward a conception of teachers' learning that is highly scaffolded by mentors and university-based faculty members, and intentionally designed in relationship to coursework and training at the university. Furthermore, periods of teaching practice take place in an environment in which more experienced teachers are constantly addressing the relationship of these teaching experiences to theory about learning and teaching—as Anni Loukomies pointed out, bridging theory and practice. This investment in learning to teach is not without high costs—the teacher educators we spoke with, for instance, noted that recently the high cost of teacher training schools has been raised as a concern in some public conversations. However, most teacher educators felt certain that despite those questions, most Finnish people agree with the important role of teacher training schools play and felt assured that teacher training schools would continue to remain well funded and central to the work of teacher education.

A Focus upon Teachers' Agency and Responsibility

In this context of relatively aligned policies (and policy makers), there is also a clarity of focus upon teachers as professionals. In such a context, teachers have agency, feel empowered and respected, and engage in their work as valued educators. In such a context, teachers can focus upon the continuum of individual student growth and deep learning, ask questions about the best forms of instruction, engage in experiments, take risks, and grow in their understanding of student learning in ways that focus upon student thinking. But, at the same time, teachers we spoke with did not take their work lightly nor did it mean that they simply sat back and enacted their craft without changing or growing. Rather, the teachers we spoke with were constantly learning, working to improve and were engaged in experiments, assessments, and examinations of student learning. In turn, the focus upon responsibility (not accountability) enabled teachers to focus upon children's thinking, the work of teaching, fueling their ability to make informed decisions about their own pedagogy and the specific children in their classrooms. Finally, a conception of assessment of teaching as looking ahead and identifying key ideas for development in the future (versus measuring what is missing or lacking) enables teachers and those who support them to continue to guide their professional development in meaningful ways.

A Conception of Professional Development as Organic, Local, and In-time

Some might argue that there are areas of support for quality teaching that are not as fully developed in the system. For instance, a more comprehensive system for formal external induction support and professional development is still in development and Finland lacks the formal career ladder for teachers that we saw in some other high-performing countries. Yet at the same time, the organic, local, personal, and in-time opportunities that occurred within the schools we studied suggests a very different conception of professional development from that which emphasizes the formal, external, and perhaps hierarchical. Reflective of the trust and responsibility inherent in the Finnish approach to teachers and teaching, this kind of professional development seems to fittingly dovetail the education of prospective teachers. The emphasis in teacher education upon teachers as autonomous, reflective, responsible individuals who have learned how to study child development carefully and deeply; who understand and can enact a variety of practical strategies; and who can ask substantial, important, meaningful questions about their teaching so that it improves over time leads naturally into a conception of professional development that also emphasizes individual responsibility and autonomy.

A Focus upon Children—and a Reflection of Key Ideas in Child Development

In turn, a broader policy context that consistently puts children at the center—which begins with a focus upon ensuring that even as early as newborns, children must have an equal, healthy start and continues with a focus upon early education for children—also may help support quality teaching. A focus upon early childhood and strong teachers at the primary level, and the concurrence of social policies that support infants and young children, ensures that children have a strong early start in their education. In this context, social policies regarding parental leave and support for parents and children in early childhood help contribute to a system in which teachers are able to focus upon the work of teaching and concurrently can draw support from other parts of the system that will provide the necessary services or support for other equally important aspects of children's lives that shape their experiences in school (such as language, health, immigration status, housing, family stability). Relatedly, it seems no surprise that Finnish teachers are selected not only for their strong academic achievement, but also for other skills and dispositions they may have, from musical or artistic talent, to strong interpersonal abilities. A focus upon all the pathways of children's development is mirrored by a holistic view of teachers.

Finally, it's also notable that much of Finnish schooling seems to reflect not simply a kind of common sense regarding child development but also that is supported by considerable research (Comer, 1996). A conception of children's development as occurring on a continuum has long been supported and put forward by developmental psychologists (Horowitz et al., 2005); concurrently, the Finnish emphasis upon including children with special needs reflects a conception of children's development as fitting within a broad and naturally occurring continuum of variation. As another example, the policy regarding the structure of the school day (Link 12) with its multiple required recess times reflects an understanding of the importance of play—and an appreciation for the necessity of healthy breaks between cognitive work for children as well as the importance of social interaction and learning through play (Basic Education Decree, 852, 1998). Cognitive as well as medical research have long been in consensus that play matters, as authors in a recent article in *Pediatrics* pointed out: "It could be argued that active play is so central to child development that it should be included in the very definition of childhood. Play offers more than cherished memories of growing up, it allows children to develop creativity and imagination while developing physical, cognitive, and emotional strengths" (Milteer, Ginsburg, & Mulligan, 2011). In the newest curricular reform, Irmeli Halinen Head of Curriculum Development, FNBE, emphasized the key role of children's emotional development in the curricular vision of learning. She not only highlighted the importance of "students' own experiences and activities" but noted in particular, that taking into account children's "feelings and joy" were central to the kind of curriculum the groups are trying to develop (Halinen, 2014).

A Continued Investment in Strengthening Teacher Education

Even in a context in which educators view Finland's teacher education system as one of the strongest internationally, improving support for teachers and teacher education figures prominently in new policy recommendations released in 2015. Many practitioners and some education authorities argue that in order to develop new teaching practices and shape student learning outcomes even more deliberately, teacher education should be revisited. Although initial teacher education based on research and located in an academic institution provides teacher candidates with the knowledge and skills needed for classroom teaching, educators argue that the teaching profession is changing in ways that call for new approaches to teaching. Teachers in Finland face more diversity in their schools and classrooms than ever before; they need to collaborate more than ever before with their colleagues; and they are required to teach different topics using new tools. The new government in Finland (as of May 2015) introduced a set of projects that represented key priorities for boosting continued change in Finnish society. Within education, the government plans to work on the development of new teaching methods as well as a reform of teacher education. Even while funding for higher education has undergone considerable reductions, the Finnish government has launched these new efforts with 90 million euros, specifically for projects in teacher education and professional development. The reform focuses upon revisiting not only the content of teacher education programs but also strengthening the link between initial teacher education and continuous professional teacher development (Finnish Government, 2015).

Looking Ahead

Today, Finland (like many of the countries and districts in our study) faces challenges that may impact the quality teaching force—the economic downturn, cuts to educational funding, and the drop in PISA scores, and pressure from other countries that are adapting more market-driven policies in education. However, given the considerable investment in aligned policies that can support teaching, it seems that Finland's teaching force should be well prepared to weather these challenges.

Sample Documents

Figure 12   Sample class schedule, primary.

Kello (time period)	Maanantai [Mon]	Tiistai [Tues]	Keskiviikko [Weds]	Torstai [Thurs]	Perjantai [Fri]
8–8.45			[alternative to religion class]	Physical education	
9–9.45	French	Physical education	Whole class time	Woodwork, sewing, knitting	Whole class time
9.45–10.30	Whole class time	French/ class A	Whole class time (Music)	Woodwork, sewing, knitting	Whole class time
11.15–12.00	English class/b	Whole class time	Whole class time	Whole class time (Music)	English/b
12.00–12.45	Whole class time	Whole class time	Whole class time	Whole class time/class1	Whole class time
13.15–14.00	Religion		Whole class time	Whole class time/class2	
14.00–14.45					

Figure 13   Sample primary school teacher schedule.

Kello (time period)	Maanantai [Mon]	Tiistai [Tues]	Keskiviikko [Weds]	Torstai [Thurs]	Perjanti [Fri]
8–8.45				Music/ Class3c	
9–9.45	Language arts/Class A		Math	Music/ Class3a	Math/ class A
9.45–10.30	Language arts	Math	Music	Music/ Class3a	Language arts
11.15–12.00	Language arts/Class B	Living Environments	Arts	Music	Math/ class B
12.00–12.45	Math	Living Environments	Arts	Language arts	Language arts
13.15–14.00	Music			Language arts	
14.00–14.45					

Notes

1. A description of the contents and photos of the box can be found at: http://www.kela.fi/web/en/maternitypackage.
2. In contrast the United States ranks at a low of 26 of 29 industrialized countries, followed only by Latvia, Lithuania, and Romania.
3. Finland, along with Sweden and The Netherlands, had the most adults who scored at high levels in problem solving in technology rich environments, who came from disadvantaged backgrounds.
4. Niemi (2012) notes that teachers had a long history of being valued in Finland, and were known as "candles of the nation," seen as responsible for providing educational activities for their villages or local regions beyond normal school teaching (such as theater performances, choir performances, or offering parental/adult education) (Niemi, 2012, p. 21).
5. One important exception to this decree is that individuals can work as "substitute or part-time teachers without tenure"—and there are about 11% of all teachers in basic schools, some even long-term, who work in this capacity. While these teachers are not formally qualified, they are designated as teachers by title and are treated the same. 70% of full-time substitute teachers and 35% of part-time substitute teachers were qualified to teach (Finnish National Board of Education, 2014a). How to address this issue is a subject of current debate, with some suggestions that the Ministry or Union create a kind of teacher registry for interested parties (parents and others) to check the qualifications of those teaching their children.
6. The name of the exam, VAKAVA, is an abbreviation of the name "Valtakunnallinen kasvatusalan valintayhteistyöverkosto," which can be best translated as "National entrance examination network in the field of education." Every university in the VAKAVA network has a member on the board that sits and helps with administrative decisions.
7. In 2015, for example, the book was released on March 24 and candidates have been able download it from university's website from that date on, and the exam (which is 3 hours long) is on May 5. So, the candidates will prepare themselves in advance by reading the materials and then take the exam; everyone, at the same time, at universities with teacher education programs around Finland.
8. Regular public schools do not compete with training schools for funding because their funding comes from different sources.
9. Dr. Markku Pyysiäinen was the leading principal of the two teacher training schools for the University of Helsinki at the time of this data collection: the Viikki training school and the Helsinki Normal School.
10. While the emphasis upon the involvement in traditional academic research by teachers seems to be a special feature of practice schools, we also found teachers in regular schools who were involved in inquiry-based classroom research which was done for the purposes of improving teaching.
11. Up until 2010, the funding for children with special needs followed a funding follows the child approach; however, after 2010, any extra funding is no longer available for children with special needs. Funding for comprehensive schools was shifted such that the funding goes to the school based upon

estimates and current census data. To some degree, this change also lowers incentives for labeling specific children with particular disabilities, reinforcing the conception of children on a continuum of development.

12. The term "first-generation student" or "second-generation student" is drawn from recent OECD definitions: "The index on immigrant background (IMMIG) has the following categories: (1) native students (those students born in the country of assessment, or those with at least one parent born in that country; students who were born abroad with at least one parent born in the country of assessment are also classified as native students), (2) second-generation students (those born in the country of assessment but whose parents were born in another country) and (3) first-generation students (those born outside the country of assessment and whose parents were also born in another country)" (OECD, 2014, p. 261).

13. The Finnish system relies instead upon purposeful sampling of children's learning by administering tests to only 10% of one age cohort per year (Abrams, 2015).

14. In addition, an advisory board overseeing the whole process includes a cross-section of representatives—again, including teachers as well as school leaders, parents, students, textbook publishers, researchers, teacher educators, ethnic groups (for instance representatives of the Sami people), and municipalities.

Appendix

METHODOLOGY

THE INTERNATIONAL TEACHER POLICY STUDY employed a multi-method, multiple case study design in order to investigate the policies and practices that support teaching quality within education systems. Seven jurisdictions across five countries were selected for the study based upon their highly developed teaching policy systems, as well as indicators of student performance on international assessments such as the Programme for International Student Assessment (PISA). In larger countries, both national and selected state or provincial policies were examined to develop an understanding of the policy system. In these cases, the state or province was treated as a case nested within the larger country case.

The same research design was followed in each jurisdiction, with adaptation to local circumstances. The research was conducted in several phases:

- First, we conducted extensive document analysis, including education policy documents and descriptions of curriculum, instruction, and professional development practices and programs in primary, secondary and higher education institutions. Reviews of the academic literature within and about each jurisdiction were also completed.
- These were supplemented with analyses of international, national, and, where applicable, state data sources. Quantitative data were used to support document analysis prior to the interview phases, and later, to triangulate findings from interviews. Quantitative data sources consulted included PISA and the Teaching and Learning International Survey (TALIS), and Statistics Finland and Ministry of Education data.
- Two interview phases were conducted in 2014, beginning with interviews with policymakers and education experts in each jurisdiction. This was followed by interviews with agency administrators, principals, teachers, teacher educators, and other education practitioners. In each case interviews were audio- or video-recorded and transcribed for analysis.

○ The interviews were supplemented with detailed observations of activities in schools and classrooms, along with other key meetings and professional learning events.

Each jurisdictional team consisted of one or more locally-based researchers, and one or more U.S.-based colleagues. This approach provided both an "insider" perspective, and an external lens on the data in each. Key lessons and themes from each jurisdictional case study have also been drawn together in a cross-case publication that serves as a companion to the individual studies.

In this case study of Finland, we interviewed 33 respondents as follows: 9 teachers; 3 student-teachers; 6 school principals; 5 policy makers; 5 teacher education students; and 5 faculty members. In terms of the policymakers we selected, we spoke not only with educators at the Ministry and the National Board of Education, but also with educators at OAJ (the teachers' union). In teacher education, we interviewed program directors as well as faculty members and current students in the program (including first-year teacher candidates; teaching candidates in their third and fifth years in the program; as well as a program graduate).

Observations and interviews were conducted in five different schools in three cities: the Viikki Teacher Training School in Helsinki (associated with the teacher education program in Helsinki at the university); the Koulumestari school in Espoo; the Poikkilaakso school in Helsinki; the Myllypuro primary school in Helsinki; and the Langinkoski lower secondary school in Kotka. These schools were selected to represent primary and upper grade schools. We also included the Myllypuro school as it serves a diverse population and is located outside of the city center of Helsinki; the Viikki school as it represented a site for teacher training; and the Langinkoski school as it was situated in the relatively small city of Kotka (with a population under 60,000) in comparison to the larger cities of Espoo and Helsinki. At each school we interviewed the principal and assistant principal if appropriate, and at least two teachers. Teachers from a range of experience levels (i.e., student-teachers, novice teachers, and more veteran teachers) and responsibilities were selected to provide contrasting perspectives.

Interview data were supplemented with qualitative data drawn primarily from observations of key meeting and learning events. Observations undertaken during school visits included classroom observations, faculty meetings, as well as informal discussions between students and faculty. Additional data sources included the collection of materials such as teachers' schedules, teacher evaluation forms, and sample textbooks and sample assignments, as well as examples of curriculum.

REFERENCES

Abrams, S. (2015). The mismeasure of teaching time. Working Paper, Center for Benefit-Cost Studies of Education, Teachers College, Columbia University. Downloaded January 15, 2015 at http://cbcse.org/ publications/#reform.

Aho, E., Pitkanen, K., & Sahlberg, P. (2006). Policy development and reform principles of basic and secondary education in Finland since 1968. Education Working Paper Series. Number 2. Available at: http://eric .ed.gov/?id=ED493641.

Antikainen, A. (2006). In search of the Nordic model in education. *Scandinavian Journal of Educational Research*, 50(3), pp. 229–243.

Basic Education Act 628/1998. Amendments up to 1136/2010. Downloaded January 21, 2015 from: http://www.finlex.fi/en/laki/kaannokset/1998/ en19980628.pdf.

Buchberger, F., & Buchberger, I. (2004). Problem solving capacity of a teacher education system as a condition of success? An analysis of the "Finnish case." In F. Buchberger & S. Berghammer (Eds.), *Education policy analysis in a comparative perspective* (pp. 222–37). Linz: Trauner.

Comer, J., Haynes, N. M., Joyner, E., & Ben-Avie, M. (Eds). (1996). *Rallying the whole village: The Comer process for reforming education*. New York: Teachers College Press.

Graham, L. J., & Jahnukainen, M. (2011). Wherefore art thou, inclusion? Analysing the development of inclusive education in New South Wales, Alberta and Finland. *Journal of Education Policy*, 26(2), 263–288. To link to this article: DOI: 10.1080/02680939.2010.493230 URL: http:// dx.doi.org/10.1080/02680939.2010.493230.

Feiman-Nemser, S. (2001). From preparation to practice: Designing a continuum to strengthen and sustain teaching. *Teachers College Record*, 103(6), 1013–1055.

Finnish Government. (2015). Hallitusohjelman toteutus. [Implementation of the government programme]. http://valtioneuvosto.fi/hallitusohjelman-toteutus.

Finnish National Board of Education. (2007). Futures education. Helsinki: Author. Downloaded January 26, 2015, from: http://www.oph.fi/download/47651_netengtulevaisuuskasvatus2007.pdf.

Finnish National Board of Education. (2014a). *Opettajat suomessa* [Teachers in Finland]. Koulutuksen seurantaraportit 8. Helsinki: National Board of Education.

Finnish National Board of Education. (2014b). Perusopetuksen perusteluon-nokset. [Draft for the new national core curriculum]. Retrieved June 25, 2014, from http://www.oph.fi/ops2016/perusteluonnokset/perusopetus.

Halinen, I. (2014). Curriculum reform 2016: Building the future together. Paper presented at the Enirdelm Conference, September 19, 2014.

Hammerness, K., Klette, K., & Jenset, I. S. (2013). Measuring coherence in teacher education: The CATE project. Papers presented at the European Conference for Educational Research, Istanbul, Turkey.

Hatch, T. (2013). Beneath the surface of accountability: Answerability, respon-sibility and capacity-building in recent educational reforms in Norway. *Journal of Educational Change*, 14(1), 1–15.

Hatch, T. (2014). Assessment in Finland: Steering, Seeing and Selection. International Education News. Downloaded June 20, 2014 from: https://internationalednews.com/2014/06/09/assessment-in-finland-steering-seeing-and-selection/.

Hatch, T. (2015). Coherence, connections and common understanding in the Common Core. In J. A. Supovitz & J. P. Spillane, *Challenging standards: Navigating conflict and building capacity in the era of the Common Core.* Lanham, MD: Rowman & Littlefield.

Hatch, T., & Hammerness, K. (2014a). Individual and collective professional development in Finland. International Education News, blog posted on May 30, 2014, available at: http://internationalednews.com/2014/05/30/individual-and-collective-professional-development-in-finland/.

Hatch, T., & Hammerness, K. (2014b). The Finnish core curriculum renewal. International Education News, blog posted on June 17, 2014, and avail-able at: http://internationalednews.com/2014/06/17/the-finnish-core-curriculum-renewal/.

Heikonen, L., Pietarinen, J., Pyhältö, K., Toom, A., & Soini, T. (in press). Early career teachers' sense of professional agency in the classroom: Associa-tions with turnover intentions and perceived inadequacy in teacher-student interaction. *Asia-Pacific Journal of Teacher Education*.

Hökkä, P., & Eteläpelto, A. (2014). Seeking new perspectives on the develop-ment of teacher education—A study of the Finnish context. *Journal of Teacher Education*, 65(1), 39–52.

Itkonen, T., & Jahnukainen, M. (2007). An analysis of accountability policies in Finland and the United States. *International Journal of Disability, Development and Education*, 54(1), 5–23. http://cirrie.buffalo.edu/database/68962/.

Jahnukainen, M., & Korhonen, A. (2003). Integration of students with severe and profound intellectual disabilities into the comprehensive school system: Teachers' perceptions of the education reform in Finland. *International Journal of Disability, Development and Education*, 50(2), 169–180.

Jakku-Sihvonen, R., & Niemi, H. (2006). Introduction to the Finnish education system and teachers' work. In R. Jakku-Sihvonen & H. Niemi (Eds.), *Research-based teacher education in Finland—Reflections by Finnish teacher educators* (pp. 7–16). Turku: Finnish Educational Research Association.

Johnson, S. M., & the Project on the Next Generation of Teachers. (2007). *Finders and keepers: Helping new teachers survive and thrive in our schools*. San Francisco: Jossey-Bass.

Jokinen, H., Taajamo, M., Miettinen, M., Weissmann, K., Honkimäki, S., Valkonen, S., & Välijärvi, J. (2013). Pedagoginen asiantuntijuus liikkeessä—hankkeen tulokset [Mobility among pedagogical experts—Research findings]. University of Jyväskylä. Finnish Institute of Educational Research. Reports, 50.

Kämppi, K., Välimaa, R., Ojala, K., Tynjälä, J., Haapasalo, I., Villberg, J., & Kannas, L. (2012). *Koulukokemusten kansainvälistä vertailua 2010 sekä muutokset Suomessa ja Pohjoismaissa 1994–2010–who-koululaistutkimus (HBSC-study)* [International comparison of school experiences 2010 and changes in Finland and Nordic Countries in 1994–2010—WHO student research (HBSC-study)]. Helsinki: National Board of Education of Finland.

Kansanen, P. (2007). Research-based teacher education. In R. Jakku-Sihvonen & H. Niemi (Eds.), *Education as a societal contributor: Reflections by Finnish educationalists* (pp. 131–146). Frankfurt am Nain: Peter Lang.

Kansanen, P. (2012). Mikä tekee opettajankoulutuksesta akateemisen? [What makes teacher training academic?]. *Kasvatus & Aika*, 6(2), 37–51.

Klette, K., Hammerness, K., Jenset, I. & Bergem, O. C. (2013). Measuring coherence across teacher education programs in Finland, Norway, Chile, Cuba, and the United States. Symposium session presented at the European Conference on Educational Research, Istanbul, Turkey.

Krokfors, L. (2007). Two-fold role of reflective pedagogical practice in research-based teacher education. In R. Jakku-Sihvonen & H. Niemi (Eds.), *Education as a societal contributor* (pp. 147–160). Frankfurt am Main: Peter Lang.

Kumpulainen, K., & Lankinen, T. (2012). Striving for educational equity and excellence: Evaluation and assessment in Finnish basic education. In H. Niemi, A. Toom, & A. Kalloniemi (Eds.), *Miracle of education: The principles and practices of teaching and learning in Finnish schools* (pp. 69–82). Rotterdam: Sense Publishers.

Laki kunnallisesta viranhalitijasta 11.4.2003/304.

Laukkanen, R. (2008). Finnish strategy for high-level education for all. In N. C. Soguel & P. Jaccard (Eds.), *Governance and performance of education systems*. Springer.

Lavonen, J. (2008). Reasons behind Finnish students' success in the PISA Scientific Literacy Assessment. University of Helsinki, Finland. Retrieved September 21, 2014, from http://www.oph.fi/info/finlandinpisastudies/conference2008/science_results_and_reasons.pdf.

Lee, H. (2014, June 4). Why Finnish babies sleep in boxes. BBC News Magazine. Downloaded October 29, 2014, from: http://www.bbc.com/news/magazine-22751415.

Liiten, M. (2004, February 11). Ykkössuosikki: Oppetajan ammatti [Top favorite: Teaching profession.] *Helsingin Sanomat* (2004).

Martin, A., & Pennanen, M. (2015). Mobility and transition of pedagogical expertise in Finland. Finnish Institute for Educational Research, Report #51, Jyväskylä, Finnish Institute for Educational Research, University of Jyväskylä.

Milteer, R. & Ginsburg, K.R. (2011). The importance of play in promoting healthy child development and maintaining strong parent-child bond: focus on poverty. Pediatrics. Downloaded June 21, 2014 from: http://pediatrics.aappublications.org/content/early/2011/12/21/peds.2011-2953

Ministry of Education and Culture. (2012). Education and research 2011–2016. A development plan. Reports of the Ministry of Education and Culture, Finland. 2012:3. Retrieved from http://www.minedu.fi/OPM/Julkaisut/2012/Kehittamissuunnitelma.html?lang=fi&extra_locale=en.

Ministry of Education and Culture, Finland. Press release on PISA 2012 results: PISA 2012: Proficiency of Finnish Youth Declining. http://www.minedu.fi/OPM/Tiedotteet/2013/12/pisa.html?lang=en.

Ministry of Education and Culture, Finland. (August 10, 2013). Press release, "Basic skills of Finnish adults one of the best in the OECD countries." http://www.minedu.fi/OPM/Tiedotteet/2013/10/piaac2013.html?lang=en.

Milteer, R., Ginsburg, K. R., & Mulligan, D.A. (2011). The importance of play in promoting healthy child development and maintaining strong parent-child bond: Focus on children in poverty. Published online December 26, 2011. *Pediatrics*, 129(1), e204–e213 (doi: 10.1542/peds.2011-2953)

McWayne C. M., Fantuzzo J. W., McDermott P. A. (2004). Preschool competency in context: An investigation of the unique contribution of child competencies to early academic success. *Developmental Psychology* 40(4), 633–645.

National Core Curriculum for Basic Education. (2004). Amendments and additions valid from 1.1.2011. http://www.oph.fi/english/curricula_and_qualifications/basic_education.

Niemi, H. (2012). The societal factors. In H. Niemi, A. Toom, & A. Kallioniemi (Eds). (2012). *Miracle of education: The principles and practices of teaching and learning in Finnish schools.* Rotterdam, The Netherlands: Sense Publishers.

Niemi, H., Toom, A., & Kallioniemi, A. (Eds). (2012). *Miracle of education: The principles and practices of teaching and learning in Finnish schools.* Rotterdam, The Netherlands: Sense Publishers.

OECD (2011). Indicator D3: how much are teachers paid? in Education at a Glance: OECD indicators. OECD Publishing.

OECD. (2014c). *Talis 2013 Results: an international perspective on teaching and learning*, OECD Publishing. http://dx.doi.org/10.1787/9789264196261-en.

OECD. (2012). *Education at a glance 2012: OECD indicators*, OECD Publishing. http://dx.doi.org/10.1787/eag-2012-en.

OECD. (2013a). *OECD skills outlook 2013: First results from the survey of adult skills*, OECD Publishing. http://dx.doi.org/10.1787/9789264204256-en.

OECD. (2013b). Teachers' salaries, *Government at a glance 2013*, OECD Publishing. Downloaded March 4, 2014, from http://dx.doi.org/10.1787/gov_glance-2013-39-en.

OECD. (2014a). Doctors and nurses salary information. Downloaded February 25, 2014, from: http://www.oecd-ilibrary.org/sites/gov_glance-2011-en/06/02/index.html?itemId=/content/chapter/gov_glance-2011-32-en.

OECD. (2014b). Teacher salary table. Downloaded February 25, 2014, at: http://www.oecd-ilibrary.org/education/teachers-salaries_teachsal-table-en.

Paksuniemi, M. (2009). *Tornion alakansakoulunopettajaseminaarin opettajakuva lukuvuosina 1921–1945 rajautuen oppilasvalintoihin, oppikirjoihin ja oheistoimintaan* [The teacher image in the lower primary school teachers' college of Tornio in 1921–1945 in the light of selection of students, textbooks, and activities of leisure time]. (PhD diss., University of Lapland, Rovaniemi, Finland).

Piesanen, E., Kiviniemi, U., & Valkonen, S. (2007). [Follow up and evaluation of the teacher education development program: Continuing teacher education in 2005 and it's follow up 1998–2005 by fields and subjects in different types of educational institutions.] Jyväskylä: University of Jyväskylä, Institute for Education Research.

Rinne, R., Kivirauma, J., & Lehtinen, E. (2004). *Johdatus kasvatustieteisiin*. Porvoo: WSOY.

Sabel, C., Saxenian, A. L., Miettinen, R., Kristensen, P. H., & Hautamäki, J. (2010). Individualized service provision in the new welfare state: Lessons from special education in Finland. Report Prepared for SITRA. Helsinki.

Sahlberg, P. (2011). *Finnish lessons: What can the world learn from educational change in Finland?* New York: Teachers College Press.

Sahlberg, P. (2015). *Finnish lessons 2.0: What can the world learn from education in Finland?* New York: Teachers College Press.

Shulman, L. S. (1986). Those who understand: Knowledge growth in teaching. *Educational Researcher*, 15(2), 4–14.

Shulman, L. S. (2000). From Minsk to Pinsk: Why a scholarship of teaching and learning? Published in the first issue of *The Journal of the Scholarship of Teaching and Learning* (JoSoTL), and based on a presentation to the American Association for Higher Education (AAHE) at its 2000 annual meeting in Anaheim, CA.

Statistics Finland. (2013). Downloaded January 20, 2015, from: http://tilastokeskus.fi/til/kou_en.html.

Statistics Finland. (June 12, 2014a). Share of students having received special support diminished. https://www.stat.fi/til/erop/index_en.html.

Statistics Finland. (2014b). Downloaded January 20, 2015, from: http://tilastokeskus.fi/til/kou_en.html.

Statistics Finland. (2015). Educational structure of population. Downloaded January 26, 2105, from: http://www.stat.fi/til/vkour/index_en.html.

Thuneberg, H., Hautamäki, J., Ahtiainen, R., Lintuvuori, M., Vainikainen, M-P., & Hilasvuori, T. (2014). Conceptual change in adopting the nationwide special education strategy in Finland. *Journal of Educational Change*, 15(1), 37–56.

Thuneberg, H., Vainikainen, M-P., Ahtiainen, R., Lintuvuori, M., Salo, K., & Hautamäki, J. (2013). Education is special for all—the Finnish support model. *Gemeinsam Leben*, 21(2), 65–78.

Toom, A., Kynäslahti, H., Krokfors, L., Jyrhämä, R., Byman, R., Stenberg, K., Maaranen, K., & Kansanen, P. (2010). Experiences of research-based approach to teacher education: Suggestions for future policies. *European Journal of Education*, 45(2), 331–344.

Tuunainen, K. (1994). Country briefing: Special education in Finland. *European Journal of Special Needs Education*, 9, 189–198.

UNICEF Innocenti Research Centre. (2007). Child poverty in perspective: An overview of child well-being in rich countries, Report Card 7, (UNICEF).

UNICEF Office of Research. (2013). Child well-being in rich countries: A comparative overview, *Innocenti Report Card 11*, UNICEF Office of Research, Florence.

United Nations. (2014). *Human development report 2014: Sustaining human progress: Reducing vulnerabilities and building resistance.* New York: United Nations Development Programme.

University of Helsinki Teachers' Academy (Homepage). (2014). Viewed January 30, 2014. Available at: http://www.helsinki.fi/opettajienakatemia/eng/.

University of Helsinki, Vakava. (2014). VAKAVA. The National Selection Cooperation Network in the Field of Education. Accessed January 30, 2014. For information on the Vakava, see: http://www.helsinki.fi/vakava/english/index.htm.

Uusiautti, S., & Määttä, K. (2013). Significant trends in the development of Finnish teacher training education programs (1860–2010). *Education Policy Analysis Archives*, 21(59). Retrieved from http://epaa.asu.edu/ojs/article/view/1276.

Välijärvi, J., & Sahlberg, P. (2008). Should "failing" students repeat a grade? Retrospective response from Finland. *Journal of Educational Change, 9*, 385–389.

Vitikka, E., Krokfors, L., & Hurmerinta, E. (2012). The Finnish National Core Curriculum: Structure and development. In H. Niemi, A. Toom, & A. Kalloniemi (Eds.), *Miracle of education: The principles and practices of teaching and learning in Finnish schools* (pp. 83–96). Rotterdam: Sense Publishers.